THE
5
minute
CLEAN
ROUTINE

Tips and tricks for a happy home

THE 5 minute CLEAN ROUTINE

ANNA LOUISA

C

CENTURY

CENTURY

UK | USA | Canada | Ireland | Australia
India | New Zealand | South Africa

Century is part of the Penguin Random House group of companies
whose addresses can be found at global.penguinrandomhouse.com

Penguin Random House UK,
One Embassy Gardens, 8 Viaduct Gardens, London sw11 7bw

penguin.co.uk

Penguin
Random House
UK

First published 2025

003

Illustrations by Simone Carr at Ellie and Liv

Typeset in 11.7/16pt Calluna by Jouve (UK), Milton Keynes
Printed and bound in Great Britain by Clays Ltd, Elcograf S.p.A.

The authorised representative in the EEA is Penguin Random House Ireland,
Morrison Chambers, 32 Nassau Street, Dublin D02 YH68

A CIP catalogue record for this book is available from the British Library

ISBN: 978–1–529–94198–2

Penguin Random House is committed to a sustainable future
for our business, our readers and our planet. This book is made
from Forest Stewardship Council® certified paper.

MIX
Paper | Supporting
responsible forestry
FSC
www.fsc.org   FSC® C018179

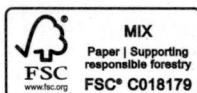

To my precious little boy

I dedicate this book to you for being the inspiration I never knew I needed, for showing me the strength I never knew I had and for being a constant reminder about what is truly important in life.

Contents

Introduction   I

Chapter 1: The Five-Minute Clean Routine   5

Chapter 2: Getting Started   29

Chapter 3: Daily Habits   71

Chapter 4: Declutter and Organise   95

Chapter 5: Bathroom and Toilet   123

Chapter 6: Kitchen   145

Chapter 7: Bedroom   173

Chapter 8: Living Areas   191

Chapter 9: Laundry and Ironing   209

Chapter 10: Pests, Pets and Stubborn Stains   231

Chapter 11: Special Touches   255

Chapter 12: Create Your Own Five-Minute
            Clean Routine   275

Conclusion   289
Notes   291
Checklist   297
Calendar   303
Acknowledgements   311
Index   313

INTRODUCTION

Hello! I'm Anna Louisa, home bird, parent and creator of cleaning, interior design and lifestyle hacks. I am so excited now to put everything I've learnt in a book. It's packed full of cleaning tips, clever shortcuts and step by step planners, as well as the full lowdown on the Five-Minute Clean Routine.

I have so much to share, but let me first take you back to where it all began: my home. I love being at home, it really is my happy place. When I close that front door, I want to feel calm and to take pleasure in my house, away from the hustle and bustle of the outside world. Interior design has always been something of a passion – if I'm in a shop, I'm far more likely to be rifling through items in the home section than anywhere else – and I enjoy restyling, renovating and adding little touches to my surroundings so that my home feels like my space, a place where I can breathe.

I started sharing DIY projects, kitchen makeovers and ideas for simple decor on Instagram. I worked as a teacher so I didn't have many spare hours to spend on projects, but I thought it would be fun to share my house renovation journey with my friends, family and – to my huge surprise – growing number of online followers.

And then my life changed when my son Oliver arrived. It meant I had even less spare time, and my focus switched to finding the quickest and most effective way of keeping on top of the household cleaning. I was proud of the house I had created – my fresh new kitchen and comfortable, uncluttered living room – but it wasn't going to stay that way if I didn't maintain it properly and keep on top of the mess.

So I posted more of what I was doing – quick tips for cleaning the bathroom, stairs, you name it, along with some of the amazing gadgets and products I found that cut cleaning time in half. People responded to my posts and seemed to enjoy my hacks and product recommendations. There are also those who find it therapeutic to watch other people clean – I get that; cleaning for me is a calming activity and it's certainly rewarding to create some order or scrub away grime in seconds.

I then noticed that my tips focusing on quick five-minute (or under) cleaning hacks seemed to attract the most attention. When it comes to everyday chores, people really do feel the need for speed, and I could see there was a real interest in quick and clever ideas for the home. I think people are also intrigued to see how much you can achieve in just a few minutes of cleaning, especially if you have the right tools, products and know-how.

That, in short, led me to devise the Five-Minute Clean Routine, a fresh approach to cleaning that is built around five-minute tasks and simple, daily habits. It's a system that gives momentum to your cleaning, challenging you to get things done quickly and efficiently. It's also easy to follow, packed full of incentives and small wins, and you can tailor it around your commitments and day-to-day life, whether you're short on time, working from home and drowning in clutter, or just in need of some helpful advice.

My hope is that there's something for everyone in the book, and that I inspire the odd person to pick up a mop, cloth or sonic scrubber (it's sad how much I love my sonic scrubber!) and give their home a quick clean, no matter how pressed for time they are. I would much rather spend time with my family than slog away cleaning for the whole day – and now, thanks to this plan, so can you! Most of the cleaning jobs are quick and easy and for any that take longer than five minutes, you can tackle them gradually over a few days or you might feel motivated to keep going! Just do whatever works for you that day or week – there are no hard and fast rules here.

In sharing household tips online, I've also learnt a huge amount, and love to swap ideas with my followers. If someone shares a tip, I'll try it out, and I'm always open to advice and enjoy the collaborative nature of social media. I'm also in touch with other home content creators, many of them parents like me, and we help and support each other to find quick ways of keeping on top of our homes.

The beauty of the Five-Minute Clean Routine is that it can fit around your life or be woven into the constant daily juggle, which might be even more challenging if you have physical limitations or find cleaning or life overwhelming at times – I know I do. There's so much in the book, from how to build good daily habits, to tips on decluttering and prepping for the next day, as well as ways to make your home feel and smell amazing. And if you love a checklist, then this is the right place for you, plus I've included weekly, monthly and seasonal planners which I know many people find useful.

Whether you're chomping at the bit to clean or desperate for some motivation, I hope you enjoy the Five-Minute Clean Routine. Grab a cloth, mop or squeegee and off you go – it's only for five minutes, so what's stopping you?

CHAPTER 1

THE FIVE-MINUTE
CLEAN ROUTINE

This chapter outlines the concept of the Five-Minute Clean Routine, how it helped me through difficult times and why it works. I'll show how it can provide momentum to your cleaning, how it can benefit and reward you, *and* fit around your commitments. There's also a fun questionnaire at the end to help you figure out what you want to achieve with your cleaning, as well as a five-minute challenge to kick-start the whole process.

I've always liked a routine to my day. As a primary school teacher, my life revolved around a timetable, a structure that worked well with the children and which suited me down to the ground. Then, when I took a break from work after having my son Oliver, much as I loved being with him, I missed that set routine. The thought of the day stretching before me felt, if I'm honest, a little overwhelming. I knew I needed to take back control.

So I set about implementing a routine at home. Oliver was my priority, so everything had to work around him, but I needed to figure out a way to keep on top of the housework and enjoy the extra time I had at home with my family. Looking after a baby meant tackling tasks in short bursts. Oliver didn't nap much during the day, just fifteen to twenty minutes at a time in the early days, and a maximum of thirty minutes in the morning and afternoon when he was a bit older. I found myself scrabbling to get things done in those brief windows of time, cleaning as quickly as I could and trying to fit in a little bit of rest between the chores.

That 'me time' was particularly important as I've always been prone to anxiety. I've learnt to manage it, but a routine really helps: it gives a structure and solidity to the day, especially when making even the most straightforward decision can seem almost impossible. With a baby to look after, I needed to keep things simple: put away the laundry, fill the dishwasher, wipe the worktops – five-minute tasks that were easy to achieve and made the house look and feel a little bit better. That, in turn, meant I wasn't waking up to chaos the next morning, which put me in a better frame of mind for the day ahead. Those small, seemingly insignificant tasks made a difference and the repetition of them soothed me.

My routine also involved making checklists of things I wanted to do. Even today, I have a little notepad by my bed and before going to sleep I make a list for the next day. It can include anything, from cleaning tasks to errands I need to run or people I need to call. I find it's a way of unloading my brain, or at least untangling some of the thoughts racing through my mind, so I'm not constantly churning over them when I should be sleeping.

The joy of lists is not just creating them but also ticking off the items as you do them. It's there in black and white (or pink, green, whatever floats your boat) – you did that thing. The task may be tiny – book a doctor's appointment or clean out the junk drawer – but it's a small, satisfying win, which has an impact and makes you feel like you're in the driving seat of your own life rather than a back-seat passenger.

Many of the tasks on my to-do list were simple, five-minute jobs, which I could weave around Oliver's needs and whatever else I wanted to do that day. It was then I realised that most household chores can be achieved in minutes, or at least broken down into manageable chunks of time.

As a teacher, I was used to setting simple tasks for my

primary school pupils, ones that could be achieved in just a few minutes – any longer and they'd lose interest. For the children who performed their tasks well, there would be some kind of reward – an extra five minutes of play or responsibility – any small incentive that would help to keep them motivated and focused. And then of course there were those chores that I tried to make as fun as possible – so much so that many of the children in my class were desperate to be chosen to wash up the art materials. Wear a colourful apron and splash about in warm soapy water? Yes please!

Us adults are not so very different to children: we respond to incentives, we like to be challenged, and sometimes even enjoy the odd chore. Some of us also struggle to get going or stick with a task and can be easily distracted, by our phones, work, or all manner of things. We have moods, good days and bad days, and emotions can inform our decisions and what we choose to do with our time. We are adults, yes, but we share many of the same impulses of children; we can't help it, we're just built that way!

Developing a routine that taps into the instincts we all share seemed to me a no-brainer. My thinking was that quick and effective bouts of cleaning would surely be more attainable, and appealing, than hours of chores, as would a routine made up of small wins and rewards. Anything that doesn't feel like a 'chore' has got to be good, and quick tidy-ups that become automatic and often take seconds are a key part of the Five-Minute Clean Routine and can make a big impact in your home in the long term.

So, what is the Five-Minute Clean Routine? It builds on the concept of quick bursts of cleaning, which evolve into everyday habits, combined with weekly, monthly and seasonal tasks – all outlined in this book – to create a routine that works for you.

The five-minute challenge

To get started on the routine, why not see for yourself how much you can achieve in just five minutes of cleaning. Choose a room or area – it could be your living room or kitchen – then set a timer and clean for five minutes exactly. In the living room, you might give the floor a quick vacuum, plump up the cushions and remove any dirty crockery. In the kitchen you could give the worktops a clean, put away some dishes or wipe down the kettle or toaster – it's up to you. Just make quick decisions during those five minutes, keep going and remain focused on the job.

When your five minutes are up, take a look at what you've achieved. You could even take a before and after picture as visible evidence of the difference. Do the rooms look a little tidier, more organised and pleasing to the eye? Does the result surprise you? How does it make you feel?

Over the next few days, repeat those five-minute sessions in other rooms or areas. What could you achieve in the entrance way of your home, or in a bathroom or bedroom? After just a few sessions, does your home feel a little more ordered? Were some areas easier to clean than others?

Here's an example of what you could achieve in five minutes in each room or area of your home:

Living room – vacuum floor, dust, plump cushions, remove crockery

Kitchen – empty dishwasher, wipe worktops or sink

Bathroom – clean sink, toilet, shower screen or mirrors

- Master bedroom – put away clothes, tidy side tables, dust surfaces
- Kids' bedroom – tidy away clothes, vacuum floor
- Laundry/utility room – hang up wet clothes, wipe surfaces

These initial five-minute challenges are a great way to kick-start this new approach to cleaning. You could do one five-minute challenge or several sessions, after which you might feel more on top of your cleaning, or at least motivated to keep it that way. Five minutes of cleaning can be slotted in easily around your other commitments, whether that's first thing in the morning or after work – it's your home and life, so do what works best for you.

Once you've seen what can be done in just five minutes, you can then start building in more of the routine, with the aim that many of the above tasks become habits – things you automatically do as you go about your day. These daily habits – making your bed, picking up your clothes, quickly resetting a room – are at the heart of the Five-Minute Clean Routine. Cleaning is a continual process – that bathroom *will* get messy again – so all those microtasks that we can fit into the flow of our day are super-important, and I cover them in more detail in chapter three.

With those daily habits in place, there are of course other cleaning tasks you need to do on a weekly, monthly or seasonal basis. Your sofa covers might require some special attention, or the shower screen needs scrubbing – all these tasks are outlined in this book, complete with tips on the best tools and products to use, along with genius hacks on how to speed up your cleaning. Some cleaning tasks will take longer than five minutes, but bigger jobs can be broken down into manageable chunks of work, so you can tackle them gradually in the time you have – or you might feel motivated to finish the job in one go. Other tasks involve soaking an item or letting a product work for thirty minutes or so, with the actual hands-on cleaning just a few minutes.

There are checklists of what needs to be done on a daily, weekly, monthly or seasonal basis, and you can then build your own plan, factoring in the areas or rooms in your home that need the most attention, and what you want to achieve. You can make notes and fill in the templates supplied in this book, or create your own, and I've also provided sample weekly and monthly planners which you can use as a guide.

There are tips on cleaning often-forgotten areas of the home where dirt can lurk, as well as hacks for removing stubborn stains. And as I'm all about creating a tranquil, fresh environment at home, I've included ways to add special touches and fragrances, from creating simmer pots that fill your home with seasonal aromas, to homemade scent bags and sprays.

There are also tips on decluttering your home. It's much easier and faster to clean a space if you're not first having to move, sort through and dust a ton of items. Great piles of post, clothes and the like can feel overwhelming, and it may be that you need to do a general declutter in your home before embarking on your new routine – but even doing this, you'll be amazed how much you can achieve in five minutes.

Momentum

Let's go back to why this routine works and what exactly it taps into. When it comes to completing any kind of task, it's often not the work itself that's the problem, it's the getting going. There are tons of reasons why we avoid or fail to get started on a job. The mere sight of a messy kitchen might be enough to put you off – it looks as if it will take hours to clean, so where do you even start?

On some days – and we've all been there – we simply lack the motivation to do anything. To begin any kind of task when you're sleep-deprived, anxious, depressed or low can sometimes feel like an impossibility, not to mention if you are recovering from illness or have ADHD, autism or other neurodivergent or health conditions. It's not that you're lazy, it's that there are limitations to what you can do, or you're consumed by other matters, or can't see the point of cleaning the bathroom (again), or are simply overwhelmed by that mountain of laundry.

What might just nudge you into action is saying to yourself: I'm going to clean for five minutes and that's it. It's just a few minutes, and if I set a timer, I will know exactly when to stop. Our brains sometimes tell us something is going to take much longer than it will. Yet you might be surprised to discover that cleaning the hob takes three minutes, emptying the bathroom bin one minute, and so on.

Keep the tasks small and achievable and you're much more likely to get going with them *and* achieve them. Success is often the result of small win after small win, not one big achievement. Getting fit or learning a language is a gradual process and keeping a home clean is the same. It's made up of small daily tasks, that you repeat and build on, and everything or anything you achieve has an impact.

Setting a timer also gives you a bit of a challenge – and just like my school pupils, many of us love a challenge. How much can I really do in five minutes? I bet you can achieve just as much in a really focused session of five-minute cleaning as you can in fifteen minutes when the clock isn't ticking.

And once you've got going, you might feel like carrying on – you're up now, so why not push on a little longer? Suddenly you're in the zone, feeling a little better, and you can see your progress – it's incredibly incentivising. You might sometimes feel the same way about going to the gym or a social event – often the hardest bit is making the decision to get dressed and walk out the door, but once you're there you might be up for a workout or enjoy that get-together. And if not, you can always go home, just like you can always stop after five minutes of cleaning. If that's all you can do today, that's okay.

So just do what you can but do something, however small. To give yourself a chance at anything, it really is the old adage: 'You don't have to be great to start, but you have to start to be great.'

Small wins

Breaking your routine down into small, manageable tasks means you achieve more and feel more rewarded. You've ticked a job off the list – you may not have cleaned the *whole* house, but you have mopped the floor and hung out the washing, so well done you. Remind yourself of what you *have* done, not what you haven't, and treat cleaning not as a relentless slog but as a number of small wins as you edge towards your goal of a clean home.

Try to shift your mindset a little and focus on the rewarding aspects of cleaning. Often, we associate cleaning with negativity. Mess and clutter in our houses can induce stress, partly because it's not how we want our homes to look or it makes us feel disorganised or chaotic. We also might feel shame about an untidy house, as if we've failed somehow and the mess is a reflection of who we are – I must be a bad parent because my home is messy – when in fact you're probably spending a lot of quality time with your child and right now cleaning is way down the to-do list.

The thing is, we're not here to serve our homes, they're here to serve us – they're meant to make us feel happy and calm, not cause us stress. Cleaning is made up of chores, yes, but you can also view them as acts of kindness to yourself. Resetting a living room – tidying up any clutter and plumping up cushions – makes it feel like a pleasant space to walk into. You deserve clean bed sheets and being able to find that coat quickly in the morning makes the day a little easier. Descaling your kettle, shining up those taps and sorting out the junk mail – these are all rewards, small wins, that keep on giving.

So try to focus on the positives that cleaning can give you. Taking on those chores might make you feel calmer and more in control – it certainly does for me when life feels a little chaotic.

Be realistic in your goals – the tasks you set yourself should be easy to achieve. Don't expect instant perfection, just aim for whatever pleases you. Your home doesn't have to be Instagram-ready, it just needs to be good enough for you. If certain areas are a little frayed about the edges, and it doesn't bother you, then no problem, but if a part of your home is driving you mad or you get a sinking feeling every time you look at it, then doing something about it will make you feel better.

Flexibility

The beauty of the Five-Minute Clean Routine is that it's flexible – you don't need to set aside the whole weekend to clean your home. Instead, tasks can be woven into the flow of your day, in and around all your other commitments. You might like to do a quick five-minute task when you get in from work, or first thing in the morning before your kids are up – whenever suits you. Some jobs take longer than five minutes, but they don't have to be tackled all at once and most can be broken down into shorter chunks.

Every household works differently. If you work from home, then a quick burst of cleaning will get you moving and away from your desk, or you might find that your family gets into an evening routine of clearing the dinner things away together. The routine that you develop has to work for you and the people you live with – there might be a bit of trial and error in the beginning, but you'll gradually figure out a system that works for everyone.

Just as each household is different, so too are personal needs and challenges. We have different goals when it comes to cleaning, shaped by our personalities, time commitments and stages in life. What works for your neighbour may be a disaster for you, perhaps because of who you live with, your varying commitments or how motivated you are. The questionnaire at the end of this chapter will help to highlight what your particular challenges or requirements are, and there's more information in chapter three on how to create the best routine for you.

At the end of the book you'll find planners that you could follow. Alternatively, you can create your own routine based on the tips outlined in the book – or you can even be a little spontaneous! It might take a while to figure out what works best for you, but keep reminding yourself of the benefits, check your progress as you go along, and remember your home should serve your needs, not the other way round.

THE BENEFITS OF THE FIVE-MINUTE CLEAN ROUTINE

- Incentivises you to get started and develop long-term cleaning habits
- Rewards you as you clean

- Focuses on the positives of cleaning
- Suggests quick, simple tasks that you can build on
- A more efficient and focused way to clean
- You can follow a planner or be spontaneous, whatever works for you
- It's totally flexible and can be woven into your day
- It's about little and often and not losing whole days to cleaning
- Gives you more time to enjoy life with the people who matter to you

Early days

Once you've tried the five-minute challenge on page 10 a few times, you can get started on the Five-Minute Clean Routine. If you're just starting out with cleaning, here are the basic tasks you need to complete on a regular basis.

Wipe clean worktops, tables and oven hobs
Wash and put away dishes and pots
Disinfect and clean toilets
Tidy up clutter
Sweep, mop and vacuum floors
Clean showers or baths
Do laundry
Dust surfaces
Empty bins
Water plants

Below is a guide to how you might achieve this; I've also added a couple of extra tasks, although you can include any of the activities outlined in later chapters. Allow five minutes for each room or task and if setting a timer works for you, keep doing that.

Monday – kitchen and living room

Tuesday – bathroom, plus an extra task such as cleaning a couple of windows

Wednesday – bedroom, plus an extra task such as vacuuming sofa

Thursday – entrance hall and bathroom

Friday – kitchen and laundry

Saturday – dust surfaces, mop and vacuum floors

Sunday – change bed linen

As the days and weeks progress, those five minutes spent cleaning certain areas will become automatic habits and you'll be able to add more weekly, monthly and seasonal tasks. Doing this, you'll be able to build on your routine, keep on top of your home and develop better cleaning habits in the process.

All about you

I'm guessing you're reading this book because you want to make some changes in your cleaning routine. To do that, it's a good idea to step back and really think about what you want to achieve and what motivates you as a person. Do you love a to-do list and routine, or are you more of a go-with-the-flow type of person? Are you looking to overhaul your approach to cleaning, or just make a few tweaks? It really is a personal choice.

The questions below might help you to figure out what you want from your cleaning, how to zone in on particular areas of your home, and how you might tailor the routine to fit your life. I've given a few sample answers for each question, but there's also space for you to write in your own, which you could refer to as you read this book or if you need some motivation when you're cleaning.

What kind of changes do you want to make with your cleaning?

☐ I need motivation
☐ I want to clean quickly and more efficiently
☐ I need help to plan my cleaning
☐ I'm generally happy with my routine, I just need a few tips
☐ I'm new to cleaning and need all the help I can get

....

....

....

What best describes you?

☐ Results-driven and you love a to-do list
☐ More of a laid-back, go-with-the-flow type
☐ Super-busy and time poor
☐ Easily distracted or disorganised
☐ Just about managing but could do with help

....

....

....

Why do you want a clean home?

- ☐ My home will look better
- ☐ I'll feel less stressed
- ☐ I'll be able to find things more quickly
- ☐ I'll enjoy my surroundings more

....

....

....

Which areas of your home need most cleaning?

- ☐ Kitchen
- ☐ Bathrooms
- ☐ Living areas
- ☐ Bedrooms

....

....

....

If not cleaned or tidied, which bit of your home annoys you the most?

- ☐ A messy entrance way
- ☐ Smudges on the windows
- ☐ Clutter everywhere
- ☐ Crumbs on the floor

....

....

....

Which bit of your home are you less bothered about?

- ☐ Spare room
- ☐ Storage cupboard
- ☐ Hallways
- ☐ Office

....

....

....

What best describes your lifestyle?

- ☐ Out at work most of the day
- ☐ Mainly at home
- ☐ Caring for someone

....

....

....

Who do you live with?

- ☐ Alone
- ☐ With one other person
- ☐ With more than one person
- ☐ Pets

. . . .

. . . .

. . . .

Who or what causes most of the mess in your home?

- [ ] You and your partner
- [ ] Your children or house mates
- [ ] Your pets

. . . .

. . . .

. . . .

Do you or people you live with have specific needs to consider, such as:

- [ ] Allergies
- [ ] Reduced mobility
- [ ] Neurodivergent

. . . .

. . . .

. . . .

What are your priorities with cleaning?

- [ ] Tidy and organised
- [ ] Hygienic and germ-free
- [ ] Free of clutter

. . . .

. . . .

. . . .

Which cleaning tasks do you like?

☐ Dusting
☐ Cleaning windows
☐ Vacuuming
☐ Tidying the kitchen

. . . .

. . . .

. . . .

Which cleaning tasks do you hate?

☐ Washing and ironing
☐ Making beds
☐ Mopping floors

. . . .

. . . .

. . . .

Everyone will answer the above questions differently. Our personalities, how we were brought up and our life commitments all vary and we have different priorities when it comes to cleaning. The Five-Minute Clean Routine takes our various needs into account, and my hope is that there's something for everyone in this book. If you're results-driven and like a to-do list, check out the planners at the back of the book, as well as the checklists at the end of chapters. Or make up your own planner, go spreadsheet crazy and have fun ticking off the tasks.

If you're the laid-back type or are easily distracted, then setting a timer and getting as much done in five minutes as you can might be just the ticket. And if you're super-busy then there are tons of ways you can speed up your cleaning, especially if you have the right tools and products, which are all covered in chapter two, alongside tips on getting stuff done quickly and efficiently.

If there are areas of the house that really bug you, such as a bathroom sink covered in toothpaste, then a daily five-second wipe of the sink might be in order, and chapter three goes into more detail on how you can weave those kinds of habits into the everyday. Similarly, if your heart sinks at the sight of a messy bed, then make sure you or your partner makes the bed every morning before leaving the room. Treat those little habits as a gift to yourself and don't hold back on telling people you live with how happy it makes you if they put down the toilet lid or stack their dirty plates in the dishwasher – it all adds up! And while pets can be a wonderful addition to a home, they can make a mess, so you might be pleased to see there is a section on cleaning a house with animals (see page 240).

If eradicating germs and bacteria is your top priority there are recipes for making up your own disinfectant sprays, as well as those that can repel insects or pests. And if anyone in your household suffers from allergies, there's a special cleaning schedule just for you on page 248. There's also advice for people with reduced mobility, and for those drowning in clutter there's a whole chapter on getting rid of all that stuff you really don't need. Bit by bit, five minutes here and five minutes there, you can transform your home into a place that works for you and the people you live with.

If there's one golden rule I can give you (okay, three golden rules), they are:

1. Get yourself a good mop – see page 53.
2. Invest in a power tool (sonic scrubbers are a dream and not too costly) – see page 59.
3. If there's a task that will take seconds or under a minute to do, just do it. Okay, maybe not if there's a pan bubbling over in the kitchen or your toddler needs you, but you get my drift . . .

NOTES

....

....

....

....

....

....

....

....

....

....

....

CHECKLIST

.... ☐

.... ☐

.... ☐

.... ☐

.... ☐

.... ☐

.... ☐

.... ☐

.... ☐

.... ☐

.... ☐

.... ☐

SATURDAY

SUNDAY

FRIDAY

THURSDAY

WEDNESDAY

TUESDAY

MONDAY

CHAPTER 2

GETTING STARTED

The perfect cleaning kit – made up of multi-purpose products and tools that get the job done – will save you time and money. I love to try things out, whether it's the latest power tool or good old mops and cloths. All my favourites are listed in this chapter, which zones in on some of the best bits of kit out there so you can tick off that to-do list quickly, but still with impressive results.

Cleaning kit

Keeping things simple is my mantra and that applies to the items I use for cleaning. Growing up, I remember the under-sink cupboard crammed full of half-used bottles, all advertised as must-have items for different tasks around the house. What I've learnt is that just a few basic cleaning agents can tackle almost any job, cutting through the dirt and mess brilliantly. It also means I'm not having to root through a cluttered cupboard to find the right product, a time-saver on its own, plus I can keep track of what I have and save money.

Many of the products I use are natural, so they contain fewer harsh chemicals, making my home a safer, healthier environment for my growing family. They also have less of an impact on the environment, and by making up my own sprays and using fewer products there's less packaging waste. It's a win-win situation.

The first three items are highly recommended – they're the gentle giants of the cleaning world but incredibly effective. They form the basis for my DIY sprays (see page 34), which you can choose to use either on their own or with shop-bought items – it's up to you. Just make sure that whatever products you choose, they are easy to use and cut through the grime, and to save time keep a few close to where you clean.

The mighty three

These three cleaning agents are must-haves in my home and the foundation of my cleaning routine. Widely available, they are cheap to buy – even more so if you buy in bulk – and can tackle everything from carpets and bathroom tiles to kitchen worktops and the laundry. They really are the ultimate cleaning trio!

1. Dish soap

Dish soap, or washing up liquid, is my go-to for so many jobs around the house. It's widely available, comes in various scents and colours, and there are eco-friendly versions on the market. The primary job of dish soap, a foaming detergent, is to cut through oil and grease from food, but it can be used in a huge range of cleaning tasks from washing floors, cupboards and worktops to treating clothes stains. It's also a relatively gentle cleaner, doesn't leave behind a strong chemical scent and is safe to use on many surfaces, including granite, marble and ceramic. I use it every day and – spoiler alert – dish soap will crop up a lot throughout this book!

2. White vinegar

White vinegar is another natural powerhouse of a product that can be used all around the home. Mixed with water – usually one part vinegar with one part water – it makes a great all-purpose cleaner for worktops, floors and windows. It can neutralise odours from laundry, revive whites, descale taps, remove limescale from shower heads, and, combined with bicarbonate of soda, unclog drains. Used neat it can tackle mould and mildew and is great for removing stains from clothing, including sweat marks and grass stains. Use it instead of fabric softener (which is full of chemicals and can damage certain fabrics), adding essential oils (see page 43) for a pleasant aroma. You can also use cider vinegar diluted with water, which has the same cleaning properties as white vinegar but a sweeter scent.

An acetic acid, white vinegar is also a natural disinfectant for some common germs, and if there's an area you want to keep cat-free in your home, like countertops or window ledges, spray the surfaces with white vinegar.

3. Bicarbonate of soda

Also known as baking soda or bicarb, and not to be confused with baking powder, bicarbonate of soda comes in powder form and is mildly abrasive. It can be sprinkled on to a damp cloth, mixed with water to form a paste or added to a bucket of water. Bicarbonate of soda can clean all kinds of surfaces, from chrome and stainless-steel to wood, laminate and tile grouting. It can also remove stains on carpets and wipe away grease marks on worktops and oven hobs.

Bicarbonate of soda is also an excellent deodoriser, absorbing and removing musty smells from soft furnishings, including cushions, carpets and mattresses, as well as vinyl shower curtains. Sprinkle it on carpets or pet bedding, let it sit for at least fifteen minutes, vacuum it up and the whole room will smell clean and fresh.

....

Safety

Always keep your cleaning products in a locked cabinet away from children and pets, and check their expiration dates. When cleaning with any product, even with milder organic solutions, it's advisable to ventilate the room you are cleaning and avoid getting it in your eyes or on your skin.

....

DIY sprays

I like to make up my own cleaning sprays, which use the above three products as a base. You can also add fragrance, and the glass cleaner includes rubbing alcohol or surgical spirit (see page 203), which minimises streaks.

Always use a new or sterilised spray bottle for your DIY cleaner so you avoid mixing in traces of other chemicals, which can be dangerous. Sterilise your bottles just like you would a baby's bottle, by dismantling them and rinsing out with warm soapy water. Then remove any plastic parts and boil or steam the bottles for a couple of minutes.

Some experts say it's better to use distilled or boiled water in cleaning products as hard water can leave water spots or scratches, although tap water works fine for me. If you're adding essential oils to your DIY sprays, it's best to use a glass bottle as some essential oils, if concentrated enough, can degrade plastic bottles, resulting in leaks. A vinegar mixture on its own will last

indefinitely, whereas a mixture made with citrus peel or herbs will last about a month. Store your DIY cleaners in a cool, dark place.

. . . .

ALL-PURPOSE CLEANER

This is a great-smelling homemade antibacterial spray, which can be used for general cleaning tasks in the kitchen, bathroom and all around the home. As it's acidic you should avoid using it on granite and some stone surfaces.

60 ml (¼ cup) white vinegar
480 ml (2 cups) water
1 teaspoon dish soap
Fragrance of your choice: citrus peel (lemon, orange or lime), herbs (sprigs of rosemary or mint) or 10–20 drops of your favourite essential oil

Fill a clean spray bottle with the vinegar, water and dish soap. Add the citrus peel, herbs or essential oil. Shake well and let infuse for a few days before using.

. . . .

GLASS AND MIRROR CLEANER

This solution includes rubbing alcohol so it evaporates quickly, minimising streaks, and the essential oil gives it a nice scent. You can also use this cleaner on chrome surfaces.

480 ml (2 cups) water
120 ml (½ cup) white or cider vinegar

60 ml (¼ cup) rubbing alcohol/surgical spirit (70 per cent concentration)
1–2 drops orange of your favourite essential oil

Combine all the ingredients in a clean spray bottle and shake well.

. . . .

DUSTING SPRAY

This works as an excellent spray and polish, and it will also prevent dust accumulating, meaning you don't have to dust quite as much!

240 ml (1 cup) olive oil
60 ml (¼ cup) white vinegar
3–4 drops of lemon essential oil (or your
    preferred scent)

Combine all the ingredients in a clean spray bottle. Shake well and test before using (especially on untreated wood). If the surface is really dirty, use an all-purpose cleaner first.

. . . .

MOULD AND MILDEW SPRAY

This should remove any build-up of mould or mildew because the tea tree oil has anti-fungal, antiseptic and anti-viral properties. You will need to spray it on and leave for fifteen minutes before rinsing off and wiping.

240 ml (1 cup) white vinegar
30–40 drops of tea tree oil

Combine the ingredients in a clean spray bottle and shake well.

....

STONE SURFACE CLEANER

This works well on natural stone surfaces, including floor and wall tiles, quartz, granite or marble floors and worktops. It's free of harsh chemicals and acidic ingredients, like vinegar, which can dull or etch some surfaces.

1 teaspoon dish soap
60 ml (¼ cup) rubbing alcohol
180 ml (¾ cup) water
Up to 10 drops of essential oil

Combine the dish soap, rubbing alcohol and water in a clean spray bottle, shake and add your preferred essential oil for a pleasant fragrance. You can also use this solution for mopping – just increase the quantities by four or five, with a maximum of 30 drops of essential oil.

....

FRIDGE SPRAY

This spray is able to tackle food, drink and grease spills in the fridge, while leaving behind a pleasant lemony aroma.

240 ml (1 cup) hot water
120 ml (½ cup) white vinegar
½ teaspoon dish soap
20 drops of lemon essential oil

Fill a clean spray bottle with all the ingredients, give it a good shake, and you're good to go!

HARD WOOD CLEANER

If your wooden floor is brand new, you might want to clean it with a specialist product designed for the job, but the following solution is gentle enough for most hard wood floors.

480 ml (2 cups) water
120 ml (½ cup) white vinegar
½ teaspoon dish soap
5–10 drops of essential oil

Mix the ingredients together in a clean spray bottle. You can also use this solution for mopping – just increase the quantities by four, with a maximum of 20 drops of essential oil.

LAMINATE FLOOR CLEANER

This solution will clean your laminate floor effectively and the rubbing alcohol aids quick drying.

120 ml (½ cup) water
120 ml (½ cup) rubbing alcohol
120 ml (½ cup) white vinegar
10 drops of essential oil

Mix the ingredients together in a clean spray bottle. You can also use this solution for mopping – just increase the quantities by four, with a maximum of 20 drops of essential oil.

See page 42 for a disinfectant cleaner.

Safety

Always label your DIY spray with exactly what it is and the ingredients it contains. Before adding products, read the label and don't mix in anything that contains bleach, which can include powdered washing detergent. Mixing bleach with common cleaning products can create toxic fumes and serious injury.

Other natural products

SODA CRYSTALS

Soda crystals, also known as washing soda or sodium carbonate, are a more powerful version of bicarbonate of soda. Supplied as white odourless crystals or flakes, they dissolve in water to form an alkaline solution that has many uses in cleaning. These include deodorising and removing limescale from washing machines, removing stains from clothes, softening towels and ridding pots and pans of stubborn residues.

Soda crystals can also kill moss and algae on outside patios and paths and can be used as a natural, less toxic alternative to bleach toilet cleaner. They are especially good in areas with hard water as they prevent the build-up of hard water stains in the toilet. While soda crystals are a natural biodegradable cleaning product, the strong alkali solution can cause skin irritation so it's best to wear gloves when handling them.

BABY OIL

This gentle, translucent liquid has many cleaning properties. Just a few drops on a cloth can make your stainless-steel sink, oven or fridge streak-free and shiny, and wiped on taps it can prevent water marks. It can also restore the look of wooden furniture and leather, and even remove remnants of stickers or labels – just dab them with oil, leave for five minutes and scrape or peel off.

CITRIC ACID

Citric acid is a natural organic acid which has antibacterial, antifungal, degreasing and whitening power. It comes as a powder and can be used to remove limescale in kettles and on taps, break down stains in clothing and as a replacement for bleach toilet cleaners. To remove stains at the bottom of toilets, just add with hot water and allow to fizz (see page 132). You can also use it as a daily toilet cleaner, simply scrubbing it with the water in the bowl. When cleaning with any agent, including citric acid, it's always best to keep the room you're working in well ventilated and avoid getting it on skin and in eyes.

HYDROGEN PEROXIDE (OR OXYGEN BLEACH)

This antiseptic liquid is a natural and biodegradable alternative to common bleach. Mix with water and spray on surfaces like sinks, worktops and doorknobs, leave for five minutes, and it will kill bacteria, fungi and viruses. (Don't spray on clothes or furniture, however, as it could bleach them.) You can also use hydrogen peroxide to remove stains on white (not coloured) fabric, white carpets and to brighten tile grouting (see page 130). Always test it on a hidden area first, don't mix it with vinegar, and read the manufacturer's instructions carefully before use. Hydrogen peroxide is primarily available online, in pharmacies or in some supermarkets in the US.

· ·

Fact check

What is the difference between disinfecting and cleaning?

Hydrogen peroxide, along with white vinegar and rubbing alcohol (with at least 70 per cent alcohol content) are all natural disinfectants, in that they will remove 99.9 per cent of all bacteria, viruses and germs. A cleaning product will lift dirt off a surface but it won't disinfect it. To fully disinfect a surface, you need to clean it first, then use a disinfectant to kill the germs and leave it to air-dry. Disinfectants need between one and ten minutes to effectively kill germs, so don't wipe them up immediately.

· ·

RUBBING ALCOHOL OR SURGICAL SPIRIT

This is another natural disinfectant and is commonly found in hand sanitisers. The higher the alcohol content the better – it should contain at least 70 per cent alcohol to be effective. Rubbing alcohol can be used to disinfect surfaces, to clean windows and to remove some stains from clothing and fabric (see pages 245–247). You can buy it online, and in shops it's more likely to be found in the medical or first aid section.

BRANDED DISINFECTANTS

From time to time I also use branded disinfectants, including Dettol, and in particular their plant-based antibacterial surface cleanser spray, which is free from harmful chemicals. I find this useful for disinfecting light switches and handles around the house, rather than using disposable antibacterial wipes.

DISINFECTANT SPRAY

You can make a really good disinfectant spray using rubbing alcohol and essential oils for fragrance.

360 ml (1½ cups) rubbing alcohol
180 ml (¾ cup) water
15 drops of lemon essential oil
15 drops of lavender, tea tree, thyme, eucalyptus or any
    essential oil with anti-microbial properties (see page 43)

Add the rubbing alcohol to a clean spray bottle, followed by the water, then the essential oils. Close the spray bottle tightly and give it a good shake to mix the solution thoroughly. Shake before each use.

THE POWER OF SUNLIGHT

The sun is a natural disinfecting and bleaching agent! It brightens whites and its UV rays can also help to disinfect fabrics and kill germs. Lemon juice will intensify the bleaching effect of the sun, helping it to lift stains such as suncream. You could also mix lemon juice with water, spray it on to any stained white fabric and the sun will whiten it more effectively. While drying clothes in the sun might cause dark colours to fade, it is of course an energy-saving alternative to using a tumble dryer, plus you get to spend five minutes out in the sun hanging out or bringing in washing. Result: a vitamin D boost plus clean, fresh-smelling clothes!

Essential oils

I love to use essential oils around the house. Not only do they have fresh, natural-smelling scents, but they also help to neutralise odours, kill bacteria and fungi, and even repel certain insects (see page 234). When buying essential oils, choose a pure, preferably organic oil, without any other ingredients added. They should come as highly concentrated plant extracts, meaning you need only add a few drops to water or your cleaning solution.

. . . .

Safety

While essential oils are natural, they are still highly concentrated so they can be potent. They shouldn't be ingested or used directly on the skin, and should always be diluted with liquid and kept away from children. If pregnant, consult your doctor before using them. Also be cautious with their use around pets – the smell can be overpowering for dogs, plus some oils are toxic to cats so always read the labels very carefully or consult with a vet.

. . . .

There are so many different essential oils and scents to choose from – just have a play with them, figure out which ones appeal to you, and you can even add multiple scents to your cleaning sprays. Here are the ones I like:

ORANGE AND LEMON OILS

The citrus smell of orange and lemon oils works well in the kitchen or bathroom. They also have antibacterial and anti-viral properties, cut through grease and dirt and can be added to all-purpose cleaners. Both are good for deterring insects, including spiders (see page 235), although if ingested they can be toxic to cats and dogs, as they can't metabolize a compound in the lemon and orange oil, and both animals are sensitive to their scent.

EUCALYPTUS OIL

This is a popular cleaning oil and I really like the smell. I use it regularly when I wash my bedding, adding a few drops along with a little vinegar to the washing machine drawer. It also acts as a good insect repellent, including dust mites and bed bugs. When I'm sprinkling bicarbonate of soda on a mattress to freshen it up, I'll sometimes add eucalyptus oil.

TEA TREE OIL

This powerful oil can fight germs, bacteria, viruses and bugs. It has antibacterial, anti-viral and anti-fungal properties, can tackle mildew in the shower and works well in an all-purpose spray. Its strong smell is said to boost a low mood and help with mental clarity, and it's great in a diffuser if you're bunged up with a cold (see page 259).

CLOVE OIL

This oil is known for its effectiveness on mould. Add ½–1 teaspoon to 1 litre (4 cups) of water in a spray bottle and spray on bathroom surfaces, tiles and shower curtains. Leave for at least one hour and rinse off. You can also spray it on tile grouting, gently brushing off mould with a toothbrush.

PEPPERMINT OIL

With a cool, invigorating smell, peppermint oil is also a renowned repellent for spiders (yes!), mice, ants and other pests. Spraying it in corners might reduce cobwebs, and along window frames might stop the little blighters entering in the first place.

LAVENDER OIL

Lavender is known for its calming qualities and the essential oil is naturally antibacterial. Its soothing aroma makes it ideal for use in the bedroom and for sprinkling on a mattress, and it can be added to laundry to prevent musty odours building up in the washing machine.

THYME OIL

Containing thymol, which has potent antibacterial, anti-fungal and anti-viral properties, thyme oil can help to disinfect surfaces and protect them against mould and mildew. It has a fresh herbal scent and is a safe solution for homes with children and pets.

ROSEMARY OIL

Rosemary oil also has strong antibacterial and anti-viral properties, and its anti-fungal powers make it effective in preventing and combating mould and mildew. It can also help to deter insects such as flies, ants and mosquitoes.

GRAPEFRUIT OIL

A good all-purpose, degreasing cleaner, grapefruit oil helps to combat bacteria and viruses and its fresh citrusy scent makes a good air freshener.

Other household items

OLIVE OIL

Olive oil can be used to buff up stainless-steel, remove water rings and scratches on wood, and condition leather, while a few drops on a damp cloth provides a gentle wipe for plant leaves. Combined with white vinegar and an essential oil, you can also make a DIY dusting spray for wooden surfaces (see page 36).

SALT

This is another natural, widely available and cheap product that can be used all around the home. It can be used as a scourer for pots and pans, or dissolved in hot water and used to soak fabrics to help remove stains, while adding salt to a wash can prevent dark colours from becoming faded. It also has antibacterial properties, and can be added to vinegar and hot water to break down grease, food and bad smells in drains, or mix it with dish soap to remove stains in mugs.

LEMON

The humble lemon makes a fabulous cleaning product. Lemons have a wonderful fresh smell, and the citric acid gives them real cleaning power as well as antibacterial properties. They make a great rinse aid for the dishwasher and can help to remove lingering food smells on chopping boards and in fridges, microwaves and washing machines. They can even remove limescale from taps – simply cut a lemon in half and run it over the limescale, wait a few minutes, then rinse off. Lemon juice also has a natural whitening action that is enhanced by the sun. So if you have some old lemons in the house, get them working for you!

TOOTHPASTE

Toothpaste is another useful household staple and can be used to remove stains on walls and the gunk on the underside of irons, whiten trainers and even deodorise washing machines (see page 221). Make sure you use white toothpaste, not gel, coloured, charcoal or whitening toothpaste, the latter of which will have a bleaching effect.

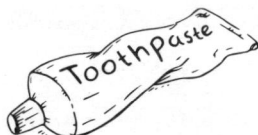

DENTURE TABLETS

Believe it or not, denture tablets are another secret weapon in my cleaning kit. They are cheap to buy and eco-friendly, containing active yet gentle ingredients like citric acid and sodium bicarbonate, which work wonders on stubborn stains and limescale. They can whiten toilet bowls, sinks and mugs, clean toothbrushes and descale kettles and coffee machines. They can even brighten white fabric by adding two or three tablets directly to the drum of a washing machine, or dissolving them in a sink of hot water for soaking.

SHAVING FOAM

If you thought shaving foam was just for hair removal, then think again as it has some brilliant cleaning properties too! Not only can it clean mirrors, giving them a streak-free shine, but it can also prevent them misting up while you're in the shower (see page 136) – game changer! It can help to lift stains off carpets and upholstery, including red wine stains, and you can gently and effectively clean your jewellery with it. Shaving foam can also prevent odours in the bathroom and can be used to clean the floor around the toilet – particularly useful if you have little (and big) boys in your home.

Shop-bought products

Alongside natural cleaning products, I make use of the occasional branded product, especially when faced with really stubborn stains or mould that just won't go away. What you use to clean is obviously personal to you and your home, a combination of natural and the odd branded product works best for me.

LIMESCALE REMOVERS

There are a few on the market, including Viakal, which is a powerful limescale and watermark remover. If all else fails, this will invariably work, and it can be useful on baths, taps, sinks and toilets. It contains strong chemicals so wear gloves when using it. Take care around plastic or sensitive surfaces, don't leave it on for too long and make sure the room is well ventilated.

SPOT CARPET STAIN REMOVER

For really stubborn stains, I find Dr. Beckmann Carpet Stain Remover a bit of a miracle worker. It has a brush attached and is fantastic for spot cleaning carpets. I swear by this.

ABRASIVE CLEANING SPONGE

Many of these are made from melamine foam, which works like very fine sandpaper to remove marks and stubborn stains on walls and surfaces all around the home. I use the Mr. Clean Magic Eraser, which can remove scuffs on skirting boards and even urine stains on toilet seats, but if you're using it on painted walls, test on an inconspicuous area first.

OXI POWDER

If I want to brighten my whites or remove stubborn stains, I will sometimes soak them in water, adding a scoop of oxi powder – I use the Vanish Oxi Action range – for thirty minutes to a few hours, before then putting them in a normal washing cycle. You can buy oxi powder products that are suitable for both white and coloured fabrics.

While I use all of the products listed above, I have stopped using certain branded tumble dryer sheets because I learnt they had a ton of nasty chemicals in them and they are bad for the environment. Instead, I make my own scent bags from natural products and use them to line bins, pillowcases, car seats and even freshen up smelly trainers. The recipes for these are on page 262 and I urge you to give them a go.

Fabric conditioner is another household item that can be swapped out for a more natural alternative: white vinegar (see page 33).

CHECKLIST OF PRODUCTS

Dish soap
White vinegar
Bicarbonate of soda
DIY all-purpose cleaner
DIY glass and mirror cleaner
DIY dusting spray
DIY mould and mildew spray
DIY stone surface cleaner
DIY fridge spray
DIY hard wood cleaner
DIY laminate floor cleaner
Soda crystals
Baby oil
Citric acid
Hydrogen peroxide
Rubbing alcohol or surgical spirit
Dettol
DIY disinfectant spray
Essential oils
Olive oil
Salt
Lemon
Toothpaste
Denture tablets
Shaving foam
Limescale remover
Spot carpet stain remover

Abrasive cleaning sponge
Oxi powder

Tools

I love a good cleaning tool, and am always on the lookout for that perfect item, one that is really effective and speeds up my cleaning. I have my favourites, from my flat-headed mop to damp dusters, which I reach for on a daily basis.

I also like a powered gadget because they speed up cleaning like nothing else and are ridiculously satisfying to use, particularly in those difficult to reach areas. Five minutes cleaning with a sonic scrubber or steam cleaner is often more than enough time and produces amazing results! They come with various attachments so can tackle lots of areas and tasks around the house, and they take a lot of the physical strain out of cleaning, making them especially useful for anyone with mobility issues.

Microfibre cloths

Made up of thousands of tiny fibres, these cloths are great at picking up and trapping dirt, dust and bacteria. They can be used on every surface, from worktops, tiles and stainless-steel to electronic screens and glass. You can wash dishes with them and, as they are super-absorbent, you can even dry dishes with them.

Avoid using the same cloth for everything, however. They come in different colours, so I use one colour for dishes, one for wiping surfaces, one for dusting, and another for the bathroom. They can harbour a lot of bacteria so you need to clean them regularly – daily, if possible. They can be machine washed hundreds of times with detergent. You can also wash them by hand or leave them to soak for an hour or overnight in warm soapy water (detergent or dish soap) before rinsing in cold water. Avoid putting them in the tumble dryer as heat can cause them to shrink – it's best to hang them out to dry, which they'll do in no time.

Every month or so I also deep-clean my microfibre cloths. I put them in an old saucepan, cover them with water, sprinkle over a cup of bicarbonate of soda, boil them for fifteen minutes, let cool and rinse. Then wash them with your usual detergent and air-dry.

GLASS MICROFIBRE CLOTHS

These cloths are designed for glass, mirrors and windows, removing dust, fingerprints and grease without any smears. The Minky M Cloth Glass & Window is good, and I also really like the Marigold Squeaky Clean Flexi Microfibre Cloth, which has a special coating and is brilliant for shining things up without the need for any extra product. I use it on my oven hob, dampened with a little water, and it shines it up beautifully without any streaks, drying the surface at the same time.

I also like to use the Minky M Cloth Anti-Bacterial Bathroom Pad, which has a smooth and an abrasive side for scrubbing shower screens or baths.

Dusters

You can, of course, use any kind of cloth to dust but I like the type with ridges, such as the Scrub Daddy Damp Duster, which picks up and traps dust, rather

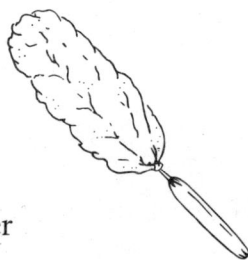

than moving it around, and can be used on any surface. Simply dampen it with water, rinse and squeeze dry.

STATIC DUSTERS

These dusters use a static charge to attract and trap dust and are perfect for ceiling lights, tops of cupboards, cornices, picture frames and any nooks and crannies. Just shake outside to remove excess dust or wash in warm soapy water, rinse and hang upside down to dry. I like the Flash Dust Magnet as well as the Lakeland Telescopic Static Duster, which has an extendable handle.

For dusting walls, coving and large areas I'll also use a Flash Speed Mop, which comes with pads for dusting and mopping. It slides across skirting boards and I often use it in the bathroom where dust can accumulate quickly.

Brooms and brushes

Sweep up any crumbs or spills quickly with a broom. You can buy long-handled dustpan and brush sets, so you don't need to stoop when sweeping, and long triangular-shaped brushes for ceilings and walls, perfect for tackling those hard-to-reach cobwebs.

Mops

Mops are an essential part of my cleaning kit and I use various types around the house. Not only do they cover a large area quickly and thoroughly, they are also perfect for getting to those high-up places. Mops have evolved from the classic string mop and bucket, which

work well in large spaces, but I prefer to use the following at home.

SPIN MOP

This comes with a built-in spinner mechanism in the bucket, operated by a pedal, which removes excess water from the mop. I use a microfibre fluffy spin mop with different heads for the bathroom, for floors and for various surfaces. It's great for tiled and curved walls, shower trays and baths, and is a lifesaver for your back as you're not constantly having to bend over when cleaning. The mop heads can be removed and washed in a washing machine, and I keep one right next to my bathroom.

FLAT-HEADED MOP

For the kitchen, I like to use a flat-headed mop, one that has a reservoir in the bucket, one side filled with cleaning solution and the other for wrung out dirty water. This means you mop with clean water only and it makes for a more hygienic clean. They usually come with multiple heads, which you can take off and soak or put in the washing machine. I also use my flat-headed mop for windows, doors and walls.

SPRAY MOP

This consists of a mop head attached to a handle with a built-in reservoir that you fill with cleaning solution, then spray on the floor as you mop – no bucket needed. I fill mine with water and dish soap and use it to mop my kitchen and bathroom floors. The cleaning solution usually lasts for a week and because you're not having to pull a bucket around with you, the mop is really light, making it a good option for people with limited mobility. It's also quick and convenient to use, as you're not constantly having to wring out the mop head, and comes with detachable heads.

STEAM MOP

I also have a steam mop, which I use more on a monthly or seasonal basis when I want to do a deep-clean. You can use them on hard floors, but I recommend getting one that also comes with an attachment for carpets – the Vileda Steam Mop is very good. The benefit of a steam mop is that it lifts off dirt or grime with steam only, without the use of any products. They're also quick to use – mine heats up in just fifteen seconds. They're great for tackling carpet stains – I'll use mine to loosen up any stains which, after a quick scrub, are gone.

Dish brush

For washing dishes I like to use a brush with a fillable handle for detergent, such as the Dishmatic, which comes with replacement heads. I also have a Scrub Daddy Dish Wand, which you can of course use for washing up, but I find it more useful in the bathroom, particularly for giving the sink and shower tray a good scrub.

Scourer

A scourer, either in the form of a stainless-steel mesh or sponge scourer, removes burnt-on food or grease from pans. They can also be used for cleaning ovens, barbecue grills and for other heavy-duty cleaning jobs, and there are many different types available, including non-scratch scourers and plastic-free, reusable scourers and sponges.

Hob scraper

I regularly use this tool on my glass induction hob to remove burnt on food or spills without scratching the surface. You can use it on any ceramic or glass surface, including glass doors and windows.

Lint roller

These come in a variety of sizes and are traditionally used to remove unwanted hair, lint (short fibres) and fuzz from clothing. If you have pets, these are a must-have for clearing up pet hair. I like to use them around the house too – a normal size one for clothing, lampshades and soft toys, and a larger one for fabric blinds, curtains, headboards and upholstered chairs. The traditional ones have sheets that you rip off as you use them, whereas the gel lint rollers are less wasteful and more cost-effective as you can clean the roller for reuse.

Pumice stone

A cleaning pumice stone comes with a handle and is the perfect tool for scraping away hard water stains and limescale from your toilet, without scratching the porcelain.

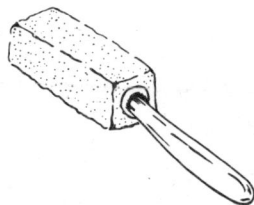

Toilet brush

I use silicone toilet brushes. They're durable, harbour less bacteria than the traditional bristled brush and are easier to clean. After I've cleaned the toilet, I rinse the brush under the flush and place it between the seat and toilet bowl, brush end over the bowl, to dry before placing back in its holder. It's advisable to spray your toilet brush with disinfectant every month, letting it sit for a few minutes, before rinsing off and leaving to dry.

Squeegee

This has a flat, smooth blade and is typically used for cleaning windows and drying surfaces such as mirrors, shower doors and tiles. It's a great idea to keep a squeegee in your shower or bathroom so you can wipe down the shower screen, door or surrounding tiles to prevent the build-up of streaks, water marks and limescale. Make this part of your daily cleaning habit every time you shower or bathe. While a squeegee is great, a window vacuum (see page 59) is another useful tool for this type of job.

Cleaning gloves

It's advisable to wear gloves to protect your hands when cleaning the house. All sorts of varieties are available, including latex-free gloves as well as eco-friendly versions such as compostable or responsibly sourced gloves. They will last an age so invest in a couple of pairs; I use different colours for different rooms or tasks.

Drain-cleaning brush

These flexible brushes, made of stainless-steel wire and stiff bristles or hooks can be inserted into a plug hole to remove hair, debris or anything that might be blocking a drain. No cleaning product required.

Toothbrush

Another vital tool for cleaning! The small bristles are perfect for tackling tile grouting, taps and oven tops, sink edges and around knobs and buttons on appliances. (Of course, a ramped-up version of a toothbrush is the sonic scrubber – see page 59 – but there's a lot you can do with the traditional toothbrush.)

Cocktail sticks

For areas beyond the reach of even a toothbrush, such as the seal around a hob, cocktail sticks are the answer.

Disposable wipes

These are effective when it comes to removing germs and bacteria, but they should be used sparingly as they're generally not eco-friendly and a more expensive option than cloths. Choose biodegradable wipes.

Dryer balls

For use in a tumble dryer, these balls are typically made of felted wool, rubber or plastic and are a sustainable alternative to fabric softeners. The wool balls help to soak up excess water and bounce around the dryer, naturally softening clothes and shortening dry times. They also prevent bed sheets tangling up.

Caddy

A portable container is a great way to keep your cleaning products and tools organised and easy to access. It's a good idea to keep your caddies close to the rooms you are cleaning, so you don't have to make multiple trips back and forth to gather supplies, streamlining your cleaning routine.

Power tools

Sticking to your Five-Minute Clean Routine is a cinch with these power tools. They're effective, versatile, easy to use and accelerate your cleaning like nothing else. With almost instant results, they're also fun to use – I actually look forward to switching them on!

SONIC SCRUBBER

The cleaning version of an electric toothbrush, the sonic scrubber is a game-changer. It cleans much faster than you could by hand and gets into those grimy areas of the house like nothing else. It makes light work of cleaning tile grouting, shower heads, toilet seat hinges (often so difficult to clean), dishwasher drains – you name it. It usually comes with detachable brush heads suitable for different surfaces and cleaning tasks. As it requires minimum effort to use, a sonic scrubber is also perfect for anyone with reduced mobility or arthritis.

POWER SCRUBBER

A hand-held device with a motorised brush or head, a power scrubber is bigger than a sonic scrubber so it can be used on much larger areas. Mine comes with an extendable arm, which I recommend (especially if you're small like me!), and I use this on everything from kitchen cupboards to glass panels in the bathroom. Most come with interchangeable brushes or scrubbing attachments: I use the scouring attachment in the bathroom or on tough stains on the hob in the kitchen; a domed head with bristles in my sinks – it's great for the corners and the sink hole; and a flatter bristled head for worktops and oven shelves.

WINDOW VACUUM

A speed-cleaner's dream. I use a Kärcher window vacuum not just on the windows but on mirrors, shower screens, tiles and the kitchen hob. It also works really well on my quartz worktops, and means I no longer have to endlessly dry them with my tea towels. You spray on the cleaning solution and the vacuum will remove the water and cleaning solution in one go without leaving any streaks or residue behind, minimising mess and drips.

STEAM CLEANER

A steam cleaner uses steam to clean and sanitise various surfaces. They come in different sizes and with various attachments and accessories so you can clean everything from worktops and fridges to upholstery and tiles. There are so many benefits to using them: the steam kills germs, bacteria and viruses on surfaces so you don't need to add harsh cleaning products; they're really efficient and easy to use, speeding up your cleaning no end; and they reduce allergens such as dust mites so are great for people with allergies.

I recently bought a Beldray steam cleaner, which was reasonably priced and came with loads of attachments and I use it all over the house, although I would steer clear of painted cabinets or any surfaces that could be damaged by heat or moisture. Using the relevant head or nozzle, the pressurised steam is great for cleaning grouting, removing water marks in a toilet bowl, and I now regularly use a steamer to clean my toilet. You can also spot clean carpets with steamers without the use of any chemicals, so they're suitable for households with children and pets or anyone sensitive to harsh chemicals.

Hand-held garment steamers are also a game-changer. A quick steam will remove stale odours, blast out bacteria and smooth crinkles and creases, meaning you can wear a garment again without putting it through a wash. They're also a handy tool if you're away from home.

. . . .

Safety

Steam is very hot and can cause burns, so keep the nozzle away from your skin and face. Always read the manufacturer's instructions when setting up a steamer and test the cleaner on a small area of the surface you intend to clean.

. . . .

VACUUM CLEANER

I could never be without my vacuum – I use it every day and it's constantly ready to go! I currently use a cordless vacuum, which automatically empties when you put it in its docking station, so is a real time-saver. Your vacuum cleaner obviously needs to suit your home and requirements – you might require good suction power if you have mostly carpets and rugs, or a lightweight cordless vacuum if you can't carry heavy items. If you or your family suffer from allergies, make sure you have a vacuum with a HEPA (high-efficiency particulate air) filter, which should pick up dust, dirt, allergen particles and some bacteria and viruses. Whichever you use, make sure your vacuum is easily accessible, portable and efficient, as it's likely it will form a key part of your cleaning routine.

SPOT CLEANER

Portable carpet cleaners use suction, brushing action and a cleaning solution to lift stains and dirt off carpets. I like the Bissell Spot Cleaner, which is not cheap to buy but is a useful and effective bit of kit and can also be used all around the home, including sofas, chairs, rugs and stairs.

CHECKLIST OF TOOLS

Microfibre cloths

Dusters

Dustpan and brush

Mops (spin, flat-headed, spray or steam)

Dish brush

Scourer

Hob scraper

Lint roller

Pumice stone

Toilet brush

Squeegee

Cleaning gloves

Drain-cleaning brush

Toothbrush

Cocktail sticks

Disposable wipes

Dryer balls

Caddy

Sonic scrubber

Power scrubber

Window vacuum

Steam cleaner

Vacuum cleaner

Spot cleaner

How to speed up your cleaning

Now you have the most effective products and tools for the job, what other methods can you use to speed up your cleaning? Try some of the following tips and see what works for you.

Organisation, motivation and focus are key, and you'll be amazed what you can achieve in just five minutes.

- Decide what you want to achieve and do it. You may have made a checklist of tasks, but for now focus on that one task and try not to be side-tracked into another job. If you spot something that needs doing, add that to your checklist, but aim to tackle one task at a time and don't overcomplicate things. One job well done – however small – will give you a much greater sense of satisfaction than two jobs half-done and still hanging over you.
- Put a timer on and get as much done as possible before the alarm goes off. If you know you have a limited time to do something, and the clock is literally ticking, you're more likely to remain focused.
- Fit in a few minutes of cleaning around other tasks. Instead of looking at your phone while you're waiting for the kettle to boil or while something is roasting in the oven, you could be cleaning the sink, clearing a kitchen shelf or sorting out some laundry.
- Choose a time of day when you're most energised – if you're better in the mornings, get your cleaning done then; sometimes it's best to get on with chores while you're still on your feet or as soon as you get home, and then you can sit down and relax!
- Listen to music, a podcast or any kind of audio as you clean. You could even make a playlist of tunes that you know will motivate you. Some people listen to calming music or even an audiobook, but I like up-tempo music because it makes me move quicker, getting my heart rate up, and is more fun! If singing or dancing helps you get through it, then go for it.

- These days, one of the biggest distractions in our lives is our phone. If you can, put it on airplane mode or out of sight while you clean so you avoid hearing the ping or swish of a message or email coming in. Resist googling something on your phone as you clean, because those precious minutes you put aside for cleaning will go in a flash and you'll have achieved precisely nothing.

Get Moving

Treat your cleaning like a workout. We're all told to move more, and cleaning definitely involves moving our bodies and expending energy. A quick burst of cleaning will loosen joints and muscles, keep you warm and give you a bit of an endorphin buzz. I'm not a great fan of exercise but it's amazing to see how many calories you can burn when cleaning. Washing the kitchen floor can burn just as many calories as a fifteen-minute fitness class – plus you get a clean floor at the end of it!

If you have set yourself the challenge of doing a number of steps every day, then cleaning will certainly help – you take around ninety steps every minute you vacuum, and seventy-five steps every minute you clean windows. Get yourself a fitness tracker and you might be surprised to see just how many steps you notch up during a cleaning session. Dancing while cleaning will also add to those steps, as will running up and down the stairs a couple of times – it's all exercise.

Many of us work from home or live a more sedentary lifestyle than we should. Cleaning gets us on our feet and moving and gives us time away from those screens. Any kind of prolonged sitting – whether at a desk or in an armchair – can lead to a ton of health issues, from poor circulation and a bad back to obesity, so it's important to move regularly.

Cleaning engages lots of muscle groups. Mopping or vacuuming uses your arms and shoulders, as well as your leg muscles when squatting or bending. Dusting high areas or cleaning windows involves stretching, engaging your arms, shoulders and core – you could say that cleaning is an all-over workout! I know people who wear arm weights when cleaning, and there are various things you can do to enhance muscle toning and strengthening as you clean:

- Standing on your toes when cleaning a high area engages and tones the calf muscles.
- Standing on one leg while washing dishes, folding laundry or when doing any simple task engages the core, gluteal and leg muscles, improving your balance as a whole. In fact, standing on one leg is proven to help with body and brain health, preventing future injury.
- Stepping into a lunge and back again as you vacuum or mop engages the lower body and abdominal muscles.
- Cleaning low spaces or scrubbing on your hands and knees is a real calorie burner and engages your back and abdominal muscles.

Just as cleaning can help you physically, it can also help with your mental health. Cleaning certainly calms me – there's something about the repetitive motion and the familiarity of it. A quick bout of vigorous cleaning is certainly a good distraction and might help to shake up your thinking a bit. If you're cross about something, take it out on the bathroom – you might feel better after five minutes of mopping. Similarly, if you've been stressing about something all morning, a quick sort of the mountain of coats in your corridor might be all that's needed to pull you out of that particular worry cycle. A few minutes of movement might help you think more clearly, help with your motivation and boost your mood.

- Open the windows – there's nothing like a blast of fresh air to get you motivated and remove any lingering odours in the house.
- If you can, keep a few cleaning products and kit in the room where you use them. I keep my bathroom mop and various bits in a bathroom cupboard, as I would rather be ticking those tasks off my to-do list than lugging mops up and down the stairs. (Remember: always keep cleaning products out of reach of little hands – safety does always come before speed.)
- Delegate. If you live with other people, get them involved and set aside time for cleaning when they're around. Get that timer going and see how much you can all do in five minutes. You could do this at the same time every day – perhaps after your evening meal – and if there's two, three, four or more doing a quick five minutes of clearing up, that really adds up.
- If you have young children, you could even put on a 'tidy up' tune. When I was a teacher, if the classroom was a mess, I'd put on a song and as soon as the kids heard the music they knew they had two minutes to tidy up. I didn't have to say anything, the music gave the signal, and once the tune was over, they had to be back in their seats ready for breaktime. Those two minutes were fairly chaotic, but then it was all done and we were ready and in a good frame of mind for the next part of the day.
- Reward yourself. Enjoy a warm cup of something, have a sit in the garden, or just remind yourself of the satisfaction you feel when you've ticked off another task on

your weekly or monthly routine. You're much more likely to stick to a routine if you associate it with small wins and rewards, rather than gruelling tasks day after day. It all adds up!

And of course, if you've set aside five minutes to clean, then that's what you should be doing. If there's a ton of stuff that needs tidying away or throwing out before you can even tackle the cleaning, then that's going to eat into your time or overwhelm you. You cannot vacuum the carpet if there's a tsunami of pillows or used crockery on the floor. To get on top of your cleaning you need to cut down on mess and clutter. The key is to get into the habit of tidying and decluttering on a daily basis – almost without thinking about it – all of which we tackle in chapter four.

NOTES

CHECKLIST

.... ☐

.... ☐

.... ☐

.... ☐

.... ☐

.... ☐

.... ☐

.... ☐

.... ☐

.... ☐

.... ☐

.... ☐

MONDAY	TUESDAY	WEDNESDAY	THURSDAY	FRIDAY	SATURDAY
					SUNDAY

CHAPTER 3

DAILY HABITS

The Five-Minute Clean Routine includes quick and efficient ways to keep on top of your cleaning throughout the year. Some tasks you'll do on a weekly, monthly or seasonal basis, and these are listed in later chapters. But what should you be doing on a daily basis? This chapter provides more detail on those everyday tasks and, crucially, how to build good cleaning habits, which are the key to maintaining a quick and easy cleaning routine.

So what do we mean by habits? Well, you've probably got into the habit of washing your face in the morning, closing your curtains or blinds at night, hanging up the dog leash when you come back from a walk, and locking the car when you leave it. These are all habits we do automatically – we don't have to write them down and tell ourselves to do them, they just happen. In fact, so much of what we do every day is done out of habit. We complete tasks without even thinking about them – but they're all tiny little actions that mean we can find the dog leash again when we want it, and that the car is secure.

These habits can also encompass small acts of tidying and cleaning, and the more you can weave them into your day, the better. By doing so the bathroom might look less of a bomb site in the morning or your workspace less cluttered when you start your day. The types of habits we're talking about are picking up towels if they fall on the bathroom floor, opening and throwing away unwanted post as soon as you get it – little tasks that take seconds, that you do straightaway or simply as you go about your day.

Some of the above may be entirely alien to you – maybe this is the first time in your life you've had to clean your own home. Or you may already be habitually tidy – whether that's a result of DNA or upbringing, I don't know – but it certainly seems to come easier to some people than others. In that case you may only need to make a tiny adjustment to your daily habits, though even small, seemingly insignificant changes can have a considerable impact over time and can in fact be a source of incredible power. With any long-term goal – whether it's learning a musical instrument or keeping on top of your housework – it's the process, the daily practice that delivers results; it doesn't happen overnight.

The habits that we're talking about roughly encompass the following five things:

1. When you leave a room take items with you.
2. Pick up what you drop.
3. Clean up any mess or spillages.
4. Wash dishes and clear up after meals.
5. Deal with stuff coming into the house.

There is of course more to it than this – the mess, like our lives, is constantly moving, and the clutter, like that junk mail, will build unless we deal with it promptly. Much of this you may already do without realising. And that's the point: the more you repeat these habits, the more automatic they become and just part of the daily flow. There's a more detailed list of what these habits could look like on page 77.

So, if you're looking to build on your daily habits – the

microtasks you do each day – what should you do? Here's a game plan for you:

Take stock

To decide on which daily habits to zone in on, think about where mess tends to accumulate in your house and what your average day looks like. If you've answered the questions on pages 19–23, you may have already considered this. Places like the kitchen usually take quite a bashing, so clearing away and washing the dishes, plus wiping the worktops, might become something you and members of your household decide to do every day.

Every household is different – if you live in a hot climate, then keeping surfaces free of anything that might attract insects may be your priority. If you have a baby, changing that nappy bin when you put them down to sleep may be your evening habit. If something vexes you, such as never being able to find the remote control for your TV, then a good habit for you is to make sure you put it back in the same place every night. Smudges on a glass oven door might not trouble some people, but if it irritates you, get into the habit of wiping it clean every day. What you choose to do is personal to you, because it's your home and life and you want to make your life easier, not harder.

Make it easy

If you're trying to build new habits, the tasks you set yourself have to be straightforward, so you can easily fit them into your daily routine. To begin with, you might want to do certain tasks straight after you do something else – after brushing your teeth, give the sink a wipe, or you could put a laundry wash on after breakfast. That way you fit in little tasks around stuff you do every day anyway, with the hope that eventually you'll do them without giving them a second thought. At first you might need to make a list or consciously think about what you're doing, but eventually they'll become part of the flow of your day.

In addition, there are some tasks you can fit in when normally you'd be doing nothing or looking at your phone. Do some dusting while you're talking on the phone, tidy your work space while you wait for your computer to do an update – little things that you can get done without really committing any time to them at all. I should have called this book the Zero-Minute Clean Routine!

Bit by bit

Remember, just a few small tasks will make a difference. Changing habits can take time, and if you keep failing to do something, then that task is not working for you, so try something else. There might be days when your good intentions go out of the window, and that's okay, just pick up when things are better – don't give up entirely.

Also try to be realistic about what you can and can't achieve. After a day's work, it might be best to fit in one quick five-minute tidy up before you slump down on the sofa. Think about when you have the most energy.

As you continue to build habits, focus also on the benefits, and congratulate yourself as you go. By keeping on top of the mess you're reducing friction in your life and taking back control of your home. Perhaps you feel a little happier and less stressed when you walk into a tidier living room. Are you more likely to invite friends round now that your home is in better shape? When you feel good about your home and what you've achieved with seemingly minimal effort, you'll want to keep it that way. And that will motivate you to keep going.

Let's go over what your daily habits could be. Remember: what you choose to do will be personal to you, so this is just a general guide.

Morning

Make bed and reset bedroom
Wipe down sink and surfaces in bathroom
Put away dishes from dishwasher or draining board
Clean away breakfast things
Put on a load of washing

Lunchtime (if home)

Hang up or fold laundry
Give toilets a freshen up
Go through post

Evening

Soak pots as you eat
Clear away and wash or load dinner items
Wipe dining table, worktops and hob
Quick sweep or vacuum of floor
Reset living room before bed

Resetting

Resetting a room means restoring it to how it was before you were there. For example, when you leave your living room in the evening, fold up any blankets or throws, pick up the cushions, place the remote control on the TV stand and remove any dirty crockery and it will be a far more pleasant room to return to the next day. All of those tasks will take seconds but will make the room feel ordered, tidier and more like the room you probably envisaged when you first decorated it or chose furniture for it. Think of it not so much as a chore but a kindness to yourself.

Sometimes we only make an effort if we have guests staying, but why not make that effort for yourself, too? It also means that when you have a spare five minutes to do more of a clean, you can focus on just that rather than having to pick up any dirty cups first.

The same goes for the kitchen. Who enjoys walking into a disaster zone first thing in the morning? It's not much of a mood-lifter, plus you'll probably spend the rest of the day playing catch up. Before I head off to bed, I like to empty the dishwasher and stack anything left in the sink. I also like to wipe down the worktops and sink so I can come down to a clean and tidy space in the morning. You might put on a little facial cream at night – not because it will give you instant results that night, but because it'll make your skin feel a little softer the next day, and over the coming weeks and months.

On social media, some people like to call the tasks you perform at the end of the day 'the closing shift'. A term regularly used in the restaurant trade, you restore the restaurant floor to how it was earlier in the evening, ready to receive customers the next day. Well, think of yourself as the customer in your own home, so have a go at putting in a closing shift before you clock off for the day.

Resetting routines

Here's a sample end-of-the-day reset routine for the living area and kitchen. These tasks take less than five minutes per room, and some – like plumping cushions – a matter of seconds!

SAMPLE END-OF-THE-DAY RESET ROUTINE

Kitchen

Wipe down worktops and hob

Load dishwasher

Wipe dining table

Living area

Plump sofa cushions

Fold throws or blankets

Remove dirty crockery

Return remote/magazines/books to their rightful place

Then when you get up in the morning, reset your bedroom, and you might want to give the bathroom a quick reset after you or the rest of the household have used it, too.

SAMPLE MORNING RESET ROUTINE

Bedroom

Make bed

Put away clothes

Take out drinking glass/newspaper/other items

Bathroom

Pick up and fold towels

Wipe sink

Straighten toiletries/other items

If you're keen to make your days as easy as possible, or at least eliminate one layer of stress if you know you're always super-busy in the mornings, there are so many other things you can do alongside resetting a room. You might search out the Tupperware for your kids' packed lunches or get their bags ready. You might make sure your coffee maker is good to go, soak your microfibre cloths, put out the outfit you plan to wear the next day, sterilise some baby bottles – whatever lifts the load and makes you feel just a little bit more in control and ready for all your adventures the next day.

HOW CAN YOU PREP FOR THE NEXT DAY?

Soak microfibre cloths
Prepare packed lunches
Chop or prepare ingredients for meals the next day
Locate Tupperware or drinks bottles
Get school or work bags ready
Sterilise baby bottles
Put away clean laundry
Locate or iron clothing for next day
Clean shoes
Do any admin needed for next day

Wind down

The resetting of a room or putting a few things in place for the following morning is a good way to end the day. It becomes part of the nightly ritual that includes making sure the doors are locked and the lights switched off, a way of putting your home to bed so it can spring into action the next day.

Before getting some shut-eye, I also have a bit of a night-time routine. If a bedtime routine is good for children then it's got to be good for us, right? I wish I was someone who could fall asleep as soon as my head hits the pillow but unfortunately that's not the case. My mind often refuses to shut down so I have a few ways to unwind and to stop overthinking.

1. Getting ahead on a few jobs like cleaning the microwave definitely helps, as I feel I can start the next day without playing catch up.
2. Making a to-do list for the next day, so I don't have it all going round and round in my head as I'm trying to sleep. This one is a must-do for an overthinker.
3. Reading. I have recently started to read regularly and it really helps my anxiety. It helps me to relax and switch off. Some people might like to listen to some gentle music or an audiobook as they drift off.

There is of course a myriad of ways you can unwind – some people like to write a gratitude journal, do a little yoga, have a warm bath – it's totally your choice. I've heard of people who, when they can't sleep, get up and do some housework or ironing, as they find the familiar, repetitive activity relaxing. I'm not advocating doing some dusting at 2am, but if that's the only thing that will calm you, go dust!

House Rules

There are many beneficial habits you can develop, some so tiny that you'd think they'd have no purpose at all, but they all add up. Some might seem like common sense or a little like 'house rules', but they are there for a reason. Choose the most vital tasks or whichever rules apply to your household, and try to stick to them every day.

1. Take shoes off when entering the house and put tidily away.

2. Avoid eating on the sofa. (This way you avoid food and drink spillages, sticky finger marks and odours. If there's no way round it, cover your sofa with a washable throw.)

3. Hang up and put away clothes at the end of the day, or put them in the laundry basket.

4. Avoid looking at your phone as soon as you wake up or return home from work. You'll get sucked in and time will disappear. Do your five minutes of cleaning and then look at your phone. The average person spends two hours a day on social media, and for many of us it's significantly more, so what's five minutes here and there.

5. Soak pots while you're eating. The earlier you can get those burnt-on bits of food into water, the easier they'll be to remove.

To keep on top of your household cleaning, you combine the daily habits listed so far with other five-minute cleaning tasks. Choose from those given in later chapters and you'll start to get a sense of what needs doing as you move round your home. You can follow my planners, revising them as you go so they work for you, or make up your own from the get-go. You might like to focus on different types of cleaning – one week you tackle all the windows or skirting boards, for example, or you could focus on particular rooms, giving each one a deep-clean over one week. There's an example of what you could do each day over a four-week period on page 83.

Some tasks will take longer than five minutes, but these can be broken down into smaller jobs, or you might find you want to keep going once you've started. Remember that it's the initiation of tasks that can be the most difficult aspect of cleaning. The chore itself – especially if you've got a good tune going – is the easy bit! Remind yourself why you're doing things: I find it deeply satisfying to have an organised cupboard free of clutter or when my taps finally look shiny and clean.

FOUR-WEEK CLEANING SCHEDULE

Here's a sample four-week cleaning schedule, with a focus each week on deep-cleaning one room. Combine this with your daily habits, plus one or two other daily or weekly tasks, and you should feel more on top of your cleaning routine. (There are more detailed planners at the back of the book.)

Week 1 – bathroom

Monday – deep-clean toilet and disinfect toilet brush
Tuesday – clean shower and/or bath and surrounding tiles and surfaces
Wednesday – clean sink, taps and mirror
Thursday – mop floor and walls
Friday – wash shower curtain, towels and mat
Saturday – clean plug holes, wipe cupboards and surfaces
Sunday – disinfect toothbrushes, empty and wipe bins

Week 2 – bedroom

Monday – dust hard surfaces and lampshades
Tuesday – dust blinds and/or curtains and headboard
Wednesday – clean and sort through make-up brushes and products

Thursday – vacuum, sweep or mop floors
Friday – sort through and declutter clothes
Saturday – clean windows
Sunday – change bedding and vacuum/deodorise mattress

Week 3 – kitchen

Monday – give sink, taps and hob a thorough clean
Tuesday – mop floor, wipe down tiles and splashbacks
Wednesday – clean and declutter fridge
Thursday – clean windows
Friday – descale kettle, clean chopping board and
      microwave
Saturday – flush out plug holes, declutter one cupboard
Sunday – give pots/pans a thorough clean, clean coffee
      machine or toaster

Week 4 – living area

Monday – vacuum floors and mop skirting boards
Tuesday – clean windows
Wednesday – dust and mop walls, dust ceiling lights/fans
Thursday – thoroughly clean sofa and armchair cushions
Friday – dust surfaces and work space, clean and disinfect
      phones/computer
Saturday – thoroughly clean stairs and spot clean
      carpet stains
Sunday – dust blinds, vacuum/steam curtains

If you choose to follow a planner or list, don't lose sight of the
fact that it's there to serve you – it's not there to hang over you or

tell you what to do. It's there to help with any decision making, guiding you through the process, but it's not something you should slavishly follow.

As you clean your home, you'll need to review your routine and make a few tweaks along the way. There may be high-traffic areas in your house that need a little more attention, or you may have allocated too little or too much time to certain tasks.

If you don't tackle everything on your to-do list, please don't lose heart – cleaning your home is an ongoing process, there is no finish line or day when everything is done and you can breathe. If you're on a long car journey, you might hit traffic along the way but you will reach your destination. If you're trying to diet, you might lose a couple pounds one week and add a pound the next, but so long as the general trend is that you lose weight over a few months, then you've achieved your objective. The takeaway is don't give up, keep going!

THREE GENERAL CLEANING TIPS

1. When cleaning, always work from the highest to the lowest point. For example, if cleaning shelves or blinds, start at the top and then move down to clean the lower areas. If you do the opposite, dust and dirt will fall on to surfaces you've already cleaned.
2. Sometimes you have to let a cleaning product work. Some disinfectants and other products with active ingredients need a few minutes to break down dirt, grease, stains and other contaminants. Spray them on, do something else for a few minutes and then wipe off.

3. Clean windows and surfaces using an 'S' motion rather than circular strokes. By doing this you're covering the surface more uniformly, ensuring you're not going over the same areas and simply redistributing dirt and grime. You can also miss corners and edges using a circular motion.

The majority of tasks you do should be relatively quick and easy. The hope is that they give you some reward or sense of satisfaction along the way. It's good to have long-term goals – and there are always jobs that take more time – but you also need those instant gratifications, and tackling the odd chore, however small, can give you that.

Tailor your habits

A cleaning routine needs to work around your various commitments, needs and stage of life. The habits you develop will all be dependent on this, and answering some of the questions in chapter one will have hopefully highlighted your motivations and what you want from your cleaning. Life also has a habit of throwing curve balls, and we all face different challenges, whether it's time pressures or physical limitations. Here's how you can tailor your cleaning habits according to your lifestyle, commitments and needs.

Out all day

If you're away from home for most of the day working, studying or ruling the world in your own way, your time will be limited.

Start with five minutes before work and five minutes after, enlisting as much help as possible from other members of the household who may not be as busy as you. Make your bed as soon as you're up or dressed, wipe the kitchen worktops after breakfast and put your used breakfast things in the dishwasher or wash them up. Already you've created just a little bit of order in your home, so that it will be a more pleasant place to return to at the end of a long day.

If you do shift or contract work, with a varied schedule, you'll need to figure out a routine that works for you. On days when you're working a long shift, for example, you might just stick to one or two routine tasks (make your bed, empty the dishwasher), saving other cleaning tasks for when you're off work or at home for longer periods.

Working from home

Many more of us are working from home these days, meaning work increasingly blurs into the home environment. But while you might still be pressed for time, you'll work better if the environment around you is clean and ordered.

Try to keep your work-station tidy and clutter-free. Put paperwork in folders or relevant files, tidy up pens and give your desk a quick clean using an all-purpose spray. Wipe your computer screen once a week and clean your keyboard, mouse and phone often. See page 201 for further details on cleaning your workspace.

Alongside your work, you could block out time for cleaning, fitting in the odd task in place of that work commute you no longer have. You could do some ironing in the time it would have taken to walk to the bus stop, and instead of the usual water-cooler break give the stairs a quick vacuum. It's good to get away from your desk occasionally, especially if your energy is flagging, and a quick five minutes of cleaning might give you a bit of a brain boost and help you to focus.

Parents and carers

If you're caring for a child or anyone needing one-on-one care, they are obviously your priority and cleaning has to work around their needs. When looking after Oliver, I worked in quick bits of cleaning while he napped, and wiped the worktops or loaded the dishwasher while he ate lunch in the same room – small five-minute tasks that meant I had just a little bit of control over any mess.

I've also tried to maintain a few cleaning habits, tidying away toys or jigsaws after we've used them or at the end of the day. We keep Oliver's toys in a chest in our living room and usually tidy them away by the early evening, so it's more of a relaxing place for me and my husband. If a room in your home is multi-functional, there's even more reason to keep on top of the mess. If part of your living area is a workspace or toy room, try not to let it take over – it's hard but a few minutes here and there might be all you need. Good storage also helps with this.

Older children and whoever you are caring for may also enjoy helping you. If your child helps to clear the dining table after dinner or make their bed every morning, the hope is they'll eventually do it automatically, without being asked, habits which they may retain when they're older. Caring for anyone is tough, so don't expect perfection when it comes to cleaning – use this book as a guide to do what you can but make sure you also build in lots of one-on-one time with your child – get out and about in the fresh air, and get some time for yourself to rest and relax.

Reduced mobility

Many people are limited in what they can do physically around their homes. Illness, old age and a variety of ongoing conditions can rule out certain activities. Instead, you could pay for a few hours of cleaning or enlist the help of family, friends or neighbours. People are often pleased to help, especially if it's just a few little chores that they can do easily.

An older person may also enjoy doing the odd chore. An easy cleaning routine might give a little structure to their day, so they too can enjoy a fresh and clean home.

Light housework tasks might involve:

- Dusting
- Watering plants
- Washing up and filling/emptying dishwasher
- Wiping worktops
- Vacuuming on level surfaces and plumping cushions
- Decluttering or organising drawers or small cupboards
- Folding laundry

Tasks to avoid include:

- Climbing ladders or stepladders
- Carrying heavy or large items, particularly up or down stairs
- Cleaning with toxic products or electricals
- Working on uneven surfaces
- Moving furniture to clean

> Useful tools: grabbers for picking things up, cleaning caddies near rooms where used, long-handled dustpan and brush, grab bars in bathroom or high-risk areas, cordless/lightweight vacuum

Bad days

We all have days when nothing feels right, or we feel blue or simply lack energy or motivation. You might need to cut yourself a little slack on those days, or focus on tasks that are not taxing or that might put you in a better frame of mind.

When I'm feeling a little anxious, I find cleaning helps to distract me or shake me out of a particular worry cycle. The physicality of cleaning can sometimes work wonders, or there might be certain tasks that will give you a little boost. Throw some windows open and give your living room an airing, sweep away cobwebs or put some fresh-smelling sheets on your bed – whatever it is that might make you feel a little better. And if your mind remains a jumble of thoughts or distractions, don't be overly ambitious with your cleaning and try to keep things simple. Your house doesn't have to be perfect, it just needs to be functional and make you feel good.

Here are some cleaning activities that might boost your mood. It's different for everyone, of course, and there's room opposite for you to write in your ideas and preferences. You might also want to put on some calming music or listen to an audiobook while you clean, or even use the time to put on a face mask – it's your choice!

- Change bedding
- Clean windows
- Water plants

- Give something a good scrub
- Clean with your favourite power tool
- Declutter a drawer
- Iron some fresh-smelling laundry
- Remove stains from mugs and cutlery
- Make up a simmer pot (see page 265) and fill your home with lovely smells

....

....

....

....

ADHD, autism or neurodivergent conditions

If you have ADHD (attention deficit hyperactivity disorder), autism or a similar neurodivergent condition, then the Five-Minute Clean Routine may well suit you. You might have difficulty initiating activities, or find it hard to keep going with tasks, so setting a timer and focusing on quick and easy jobs might be more manageable for you.

A messy room might feel overwhelming but a quick five minutes of cleaning can help you feel a little more in control. Don't aim for perfection, just do whatever you can in five minutes, and it's sometimes best to tackle those cleaning tasks when you've just got home and are still on your feet. If you find it hard to make decisions, plan ahead and keep motivated: a cleaning planner will enable you to tick off chores one by one, providing visible evidence of your progress beyond what you can see in your home.

NOTES

CHECKLIST

.... ☐

.... ☐

.... ☐

.... ☐

.... ☐

.... ☐

.... ☐

.... ☐

.... ☐

.... ☐

.... ☐

.... ☐

MONDAY

TUESDAY

WEDNESDAY

THURSDAY

FRIDAY

SATURDAY

SUNDAY

CHAPTER 4

DECLUTTER AND ORGANISE

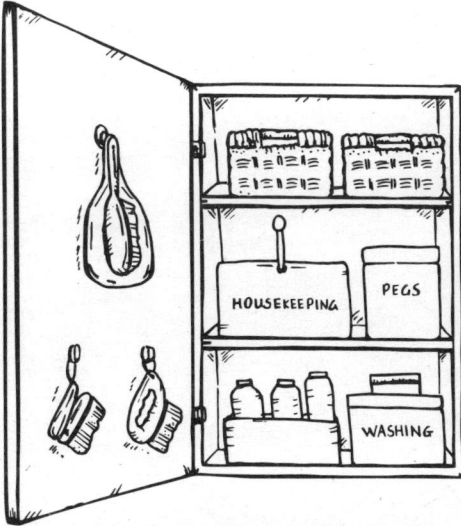

t's amazing how quickly clutter can accumulate. There's a constant flow of items that come into our homes, and the problem is that more tends to come in than leaves! Before we know it, there are trainers cluttering up the hallway and Tupperware and toiletries falling out of cupboards, and it can all mount up with alarming speed.

So it's vital to keep on top of the clutter: to put away what you want to keep and to get rid of what you don't. That way you'll be far more effective when you do clean and less likely to feel overwhelmed by the thought of it. If a room's packed to the rafters with clutter, you will want to close the door and run away. If a room is relatively clear and organised, cleaning it will feel less daunting. This chapter outlines the various ways you can declutter your home and which areas might need more attention than others.

Take a step back

Decluttering – by which I mean sorting through and removing things you don't need in your home – should be done regularly both as part of your everyday routine and in the form of quick five-minute tasks. This is not a once-in-a-blue moon task that you save for a rainy day. Decluttering is a process, something you can do every day, and a shifting of mindset that eventually results in a less cluttered home.

You might want to first consider where clutter tends to accumulate in your home. Clutter hotspots could be the bathroom cupboards, the spare room/dumping room or the home office – perhaps because that's where you put stuff when you're unsure of what to do with it. But is there anything you can do to stop that flow of items coming into your home in the first place? Do you need to change any habits here?

- We sometimes think we should fill every corner or surface of our homes with stuff. Or, because we enjoy looking at and buying home decor items or bits of furniture, we don't necessarily think through where that item could live, we just 'find' a place for it. But would your home, in fact, look better with fewer items in it? Why not clear a corner or room of your house and see how it makes you feel? Do you feel calmer? Could less actually be more?!

- Slow down when shopping. Many of us are guilty of impulse purchases, particularly when looking at items online. Think about what you buy – do you need twenty handbags or seventeen teapots? If they make you happy, then fine, or are you simply addicted to that after-purchase buzz? Analyse your shopping habits and go through your spending, which you can categorise on many banking apps now, and you might make some surprising discoveries.

- Instead of buying things, you could purchase experiences – a visit to a local attraction or a cooking lesson, for example – which will make memories and your family or friends can also enjoy them with you.

- Beware of freebies or samples. Don't fill your home with tote bags, umbrellas, make-up samples etc. Take them if you know you'll use them but don't bring them into your home just because you didn't have to pay for them.

- When buying an item of clothing, think about when you will wear it and whether you can wear it with other items in your wardrobe. Do you already have something like it and how easy is it to wash and look after?
- If someone gifts you an item, you don't have to keep it. You could donate it to charity, give it to a friend or family member or regift it to someone else.

One-in-one-out

To keep on top of clutter in my home, I find the one-in-one-out method works best. I have limited storage so I have to be careful about what I bring into the house. As an example, I love my cleaning tools and products but will only keep what I use and get rid of anything I don't. If I buy a new mop, I won't keep my old one because I know I'm not going to use it. The one I've bought is better, so why would I use my old one? If a tool I'm getting rid of is in good condition I'll give it to a friend or family member, or donate it; otherwise I'll bin it. That way my cupboards are more organised and I'm not rooting through a zillion products in search of the one I need.

The one-in-one-out approach can of course be applied to any item, from toiletries and clothes to food and magazines. Occasionally, of course, you might want to add to what you have – you might want two squeegees, one for your shower and one for elsewhere in the house. You might want to add a book you've enjoyed to a shelf – but if you're tight on space, are there any volumes you can give away? You might want to add a new dress to your wardrobe – but is there a dress you can now dispense with because it's looking tired and outdated or you simply haven't worn it for a long time (or perhaps ever)? We've all made the mistake of buying something that looks good in the shop but less so once you've brought it home! Far better you give that dress away to someone who will appreciate it and create some space in your wardrobe so you can actually see what you have in it. You could also recoup some of the purchase costs by selling your unwanted clothes online through sites like Vinted or Depop, with the caveat that if something doesn't sell within four weeks, you get rid of it!

Take a good look at your furniture: do you need another small table in your living area? Is it more of a trip hazard than a must-have item? Similarly, if you've bought a new lamp, perhaps now it's time to get rid of the broken one sitting in a cupboard. If you stick to the rule of one-in-one-out, you'll avoid the inevitable build-up of clutter that we all face the longer we live! You don't want to be that person who can barely move around their home because they've spent years accumulating stuff without *ever* letting go of anything – you can't just let a running bath endlessly fill with water; sometimes you need to turn the tap off and let some water out.

As you go

Alongside reducing the number of items coming into your home, there are lots of ways you can keep on top of the things you already have, minimising mess. Just like cleaning tasks, these can be woven into the everyday and will, if repeated often enough, become automatic habits. These small actions can take minutes, or even seconds, but they will make a big difference to the look of a room, especially if everyone in a household is doing the same. So what are these habits?

- As you leave a room – perhaps your bedroom in the morning or living room at night – carry with you anything that doesn't live there. It might be a glass, pen, newspaper – just anything that needs tidying away. Return that item to its home and – guess what – you'll be able to find it again more easily.
- Keep items you regularly use in the same place – house keys on a hook by the front door, reading glasses on a particular shelf, medicine in a certain cabinet – and return them to that allotted space as soon as you can.
- When the post arrives, go through it and immediately recycle or bin any junk mail. Place any necessary post in a designated area, and if you decide to keep a take-away menu, catalogue or similar, throw away any items that are now out of date – remember that one-in-one-out method. By doing this every day, you'll avoid a mountain of post piling up while also reducing the risk of missing or losing anything important.

Remember, try to act immediately on any task that takes less than a minute to do – those small quick wins will save you work and hassle in the long run.

Thirty-day challenge

Daily decluttering is important, but sometimes we need to purge our homes of the things we no longer need, especially when embarking on a new cleaning routine. To kick-start the process, you could set yourself a thirty-day challenge made up of easy five-minute tasks. You can create your own thirty-day challenge, focusing on any clutter hotspots in your home, or follow the one I've created on page 286. Here's a good way to start:

- Set a timer and walk around the house with a throw-it-away bag. You could focus on one room or set yourself the challenge of finding five or ten items that are broken, past their expiry date, or very worn and can't be donated to charity or given to friends. (This process might also highlight which areas of your home suffer from the most clutter.)

Things that can be chucked include out-of-date medication, toiletries, food, cleaning products, broken appliances, toys, stained or very worn clothes, pens that don't work, used candles, light bulbs . . . the list goes on!

- Set a timer and walk around your home with a donate bag. Again, you could try to find five or ten items, or zone in on a chosen room or area in your house.

When deciding whether an item needs to stay or go, ask these three questions:

1. Do I use it?
2. Do I need it?
3. Do I like it?

If the answer is no to any of the questions, then it probably needs to go. If you find you're coming up with reasons to keep everything you come across, try asking instead: would I take this if I moved house? It's amazing how decisive people can be when moving, so why not apply this mindset when you're decluttering. To take this a step further, or if you're really dithering over an item, ask yourself: can I live without it?

Try to make quick decisions – clutter can often be a sign of our indecision: it's easier to put something in a drawer than remove it from your home. Working against the clock doesn't give you a lot of time for hesitancy, so quick bursts of decluttering may help with that decision making.

. . . .

Top tip

Five minutes – what about five seconds! If in five seconds you can't remember when you last used an item, then chances are it was a l-o-n-g time ago (if ever) and you need to get rid of it.

. . . .

Short bursts of decluttering can also keep you focused on the job, especially as it's easy to become distracted when going through items in your house that you perhaps haven't seen for years, and you find yourself reading through old bits of paperwork or cooing over photographs. Shorter, timed sessions of decluttering might help if you find the process difficult or overwhelming, and take special care with anything that has sentimental value. Put the latter in a separate box or folder for safekeeping. For some items, like children's artwork, you could take a photograph for future memories.

If you share your house with others, then you obviously need to factor in their wants and needs. Better yet, get them to go through their clutter, and if it's a child you can look through their choices afterwards.

Sometimes we hang on to an item for the wrong reasons, perhaps because it cost a lot of money or you think at some point in the future you will bake your own bread/go kayaking etc. If you haven't used an item for over a year, or it's cluttering up a cupboard or the garage, and giving you zero joy, then there really is no point hanging on to that item. You could sell it or give it away and there are so many ways to donate online. Remember that giving something away means (a) you're doing someone else a good turn and your guilt/shame over buying something you never used will disappear; and (b) you'll be cutting down on the clutter in your house. What's not to love?

If you're still finding it difficult to decide whether or not to keep items, then create a holding zone. This might be a cupboard, box or corner of your home into which you put these items. They can stay there for, say, three months, and *then*, if you don't use them, they can go. NOTE: this is not an excuse to create another teetering pile of clutter – you have to be strict with yourself and go through that holding zone on a monthly or seasonal basis. If you can't be strict with yourself, then tell your partner or someone in your household and they can hold you to it.

Clutter hotspots

When going round your home, you'll probably notice rooms that need more attention than others. Zone in on these areas and break down what needs to be done into manageable five-minute tasks. As an example, you could spend five minutes going through a stack of manuals for household appliances, or you could have a quick sort through the spices and herbs in your kitchen. Just a few minutes here and there will make a noticeable difference and get some order back into your life. Here's some advice on how to keep on top of those clutter hotspots.

Paperwork

This is often the worst offender in a house. Our lives are filled with admin, which constantly flows into (and hopefully out of) our homes. If you're faced with a pile of paperwork, sort it into items to keep, items to recycle and items to shred.

ITEMS TO KEEP

We all have documents we need to keep safely filed away. These include banking, insurance and housing documents, medical letters and records, contracts, birth certificates, passports, work and pension records, payslips and personal keepsakes, such as letters from friends and family. Anyone who is self-employed also needs to file all relevant receipts, expenses and invoices.

Go through instruction manuals for appliances or various systems in your home, such as boilers or air-conditioning units, and make sure these are up to date. Apply the one-in-one-out principle: if you purchase a new oven, chuck out the manual for the old one and replace it with the updated version.

For items you're keeping, file them into folders, boxes or files sorted by type or date and clearly labelled. Go through these documents from time to time – some, such as birth certificates, you need to keep for a lifetime, but others, such as paperwork relating to a house or flat you no longer own or rent, can be discarded. Remember to shred any documents that contain private or sensitive information.

OTHER IDEAS FOR MINIMISING PAPERWORK

- Store as much as you can digitally. You could scan documents and store them on your computer, or photograph them with your phone.
- Change account settings so that utility bills, bank statements, insurance documents and as much correspondence as possible is sent to you digitally.
- Unsubscribe or opt out of junk mail – contact your postal provider (the Royal Mail in the UK) to opt out of receiving unaddressed post. Or contact the sender or

direct mail associations and ask that they remove your
name from mailing lists. You'll never stop the junk mail
entirely, but you can reduce it.

Storage cupboards

If you've been shoving items into a storage cupboard until it's now
fit to burst, then decluttering it might feel pretty daunting. You
might have ironing boards, brooms, DIY tools, appliances, light
bulbs, gift wrap – you name it! – in that cupboard and it might have
got so out of hand that you can't even remember what's lurking at
the back. Decluttering and reorganising this kind of cupboard will
take far more than five minutes, but there's no reason why you
can't do it bit by bit, shelf by shelf, category by category.

- Take everything out of the cupboard and while it's
  empty give it a clean out. Wipe surfaces with an all-
  purpose cleaner, using a cloth or flat-headed mop,
  and allow to dry.
- Go through the items you've removed and decide
  what needs chucking, recycling and keeping.
- For items that you're keeping, group them into
  categories, such as DIY accessories, candles and
  diffusers, etc.
- Go through each category. Place smaller items into
  boxes – clear plastic boxes are useful as you can see
  what's in them – and label the boxes.
- Put the items back into the cupboard, placing items
  you use regularly where you can easily get to them.

Now every time you open that cupboard – which is probably
most days – think about how it makes you feel. Do you feel a tiny

bit happier or calmer? You'll certainly be able to find items far more easily – no more rooting through everything to find a certain light bulb (only to discover you don't have any!). If you can see what you have, you also know when items need replenishing, reducing any last-minute panic.

Junk drawer

We all have THAT drawer, the one where we just chuck random items, partly because we're not sure where else to put them.

Treat the drawer like the storage cupboard. Empty it out and give the inside a good wipe down with an all-purpose cleaner. Go through the contents and decide what needs chucking and group items you're keeping. You could add dividers or even a cutlery tray to your drawer, putting lesser-used items at the back. Other things to note:

- If you have any electrical items in the drawer, such as a torch, test them and change the battery, if needed. There's nothing more annoying than needing a torch – perhaps if there's a power cut – and finding it dead.
- Be careful with old batteries, as some contain sulphuric acid and various metals which are toxic if the battery corrodes, and can even spark fire if their terminals connect with a metal object. When binning them, it's best to bag them up and take them to a household hazardous waste collection point.
- Foreign coins and notes often lurk at the back of a drawer, never to see the light of day. Many charities are happy to have your foreign currency, so you could gift it to a charity, such as UNICEF, or any organisation that accepts foreign currency donations.

....

Top tip

Repurpose the insides of cardboard boxes to make drawer
dividers. You could use these in a junk or kitchen drawer, sock
or tie drawer, or even a drawer full of toiletries or hair
accessories.

....

Cleaning products

Get together all your cleaning products and kit and sort through
them. Bin any products that are out of date, leaky or ineffective.
Do the same with brushes, sponges and other cleaning tools
that are worn out – dirty sponges in particular are a breeding
ground for germs.

Trim your products down to the essentials – you only need a
handful of cleaning items, especially if you make use of my all-
purpose cleaning spray and various DIY products (see pages
34–38, and the cleaning supply checklist on page 50). This means
you'll always be able to lay your hands on your cleaning kit, see
what needs replenishing and reduce the clutter in your cupboard.
If you have multiples of one product and you genuinely use it,
make sure you put the half-empty bottles where they are easily
visible so you use them first.

Bags, wallets and purses

Sort through all your bags, wallets and purses and decide if any
can be donated, discarded or sold online. Empty them out and go
through all the pockets, chucking old tissues, leaky pens, and so
on. Depending on the material, some backpacks or totes can be
wiped down with hot soapy water, or even put in a washing
machine on a gentle cycle.

Go through wallets and purses regularly, removing receipts and binning or storing them, and checking for any out-of-date loyalty cards. It's amazing how much lighter your purse or wallet can feel once you've done this quick task.

Food

Zone in on one area or cupboard in your kitchen. Empty the contents, wipe the space down with an all-purpose cleaner and allow to dry. Chuck out any out-of-date food – spices and herbs often need special attention, as do baking ingredients, which can spill out or lurk in the back of cupboards never to see the light of day.

Cooking utensils and appliances

Go through that drawer or pot containing your cooking utensils. Empty it, give it a good clean and decide which of your utensils you actually use.

Do the same for any cupboards containing kitchen appliances and gadgets. Do you use all of those appliances? Will you *ever* use that crêpe maker or is it just attracting dust? Could someone else make use of it?

OTHER KITCHEN EPHEMERA

- Go through your mugs and glasses, chucking any that are chipped. (See page 156 for tips on removing mug stains.) Ideally you need two mugs and two glasses per person in the household, plus a few extras for guests.
- Pair Tupperware containers with their lids and chuck any cracked items or ones missing their lids. (See page 246 for removing stains on Tupperware.)

- Go through bowls, plates and crockery. Are there any you never use that could be donated to friends, family or charity?
- Bin or recycle any worn or heavily stained tea towels.
- Go through bakeware – how many baking trays or cake tins do you really need? Are you likely to ever use those icing nozzles or jelly moulds?

Fridge

Declutter the outside of your fridge. We often attach things to the outside of fridges – to-do lists, photos, leaflets – but has this got out of hand? Does it look chaotic? Give it a sort out, discarding items that have long since served their purpose.

Bathroom

Bathroom toiletries and medicines often need a good sort through. In a five-minute session, you can chuck bottles and packets that are empty, have passed their use-by date or you never use. Do the same with sunscreens or any make-up you store in the bathroom, chucking out any dried-out products and those that have passed their expiry date.

Sort through your towels, flannels and bathmats, binning or recycling any threadbare ones or those you never use. Ideally you need two towels per person in the house, plus a beach towel each, and extra towels for guests.

Toys

Toys can mount up quickly and start to take over a home if you're not careful. Spend five minutes now and then going through them and reassembling any pieces that have got separated. You can even make this a game with your child.

With Oliver, if there's a toy he's not taken to, we'll donate it or give it to a friend. If he's grown out of certain toys, we might store the odd one or we'll pass that on. Discard or recycle toys that are broken or art materials that are used up, as well as puzzles with missing or chewed pieces. It's sometimes best to go through toys without your child; if you want to avoid any upset, you can always put the odd item in a holding zone (see page 104) and if your child doesn't ask for it during a set period, say three months, then it can probably go.

If there's the odd toy or book they've definitely grown out of but you want to keep for sentimental reasons, store it elsewhere (perhaps in a keepsake/memory box for your child) or you could take a photograph of it for future memories.

I tend to do a more thorough declutter of toys a couple of times a year – usually around summertime and before Christmas, when I know he'll get a few new ones. We put all his toys in a chest in the living room, so it helps if we can see what's in there, so he can easily reach for a favourite toy when he wants to play with something.

Wardrobe

Wardrobes can get really cluttered, especially if you tend to hang on to clothing, as I do. I convince myself that something will come back into fashion, or there might just be an occasion when I need it. My husband is much better at letting go of his clothes and will point out if I haven't worn something for a very long time, and ask if I will ever wear it again.

As I find it difficult to let go of my clothing, I make use of this hack – give it a go!

1. At the beginning of every year turn all your hangers backwards, and as you wear things throughout the year hang them back up normally.
2. At the end of the year, all of the hangers that are still backwards get donated as they haven't been worn all year.
3. Then hang everything up backwards to start again!

If you decide to do an all-in-one purge of your wardrobe, you can break down this big job into smaller five-minute chunks. Remember, decluttering is a gradual process – you don't have to tackle everything at once. Just do it bit by bit and appreciate your progress along the way.

- Empty one part of your wardrobe – the hanging rail or one shelf – and dust, vacuum and wipe it clean.
- Sort through certain types of clothes – such as your jeans, shirts, dresses – you know which clothes are your weakness and might need paring down.
- Decide what should stay and what should go, making quick decisions. You can even employ the five-second rule – if in five seconds you can't think when you wore it last, or whether you like it or not, then it's time to get rid of it.
- You might decide something just needs a quick repair, which is fine, but pull it out of your wardrobe and ensure you repair it within a certain time period.

If any unwanted items of clothing are in good condition, you can pass them on to friends, family, a clothes bank or charity. If you're hanging on to an item because it cost you a lot of money, you can sell it online or donate it and spread the love. With any clothing that can't be donated or sold, recycle it at your nearest textile recycling location.

SOCKS AND UNDERWEAR

Spend a few minutes pairing socks and going through underwear. Any socks or tights with holes need to go, as well as frayed underwear. If you can't find a sock's partner, you might want to see if it turns up over the next week or so, and if it doesn't, it'll need to go.

SHOES

Decide which pairs should stay and which should go. If any shoes are uncomfortable, then chances are they'll always be uncomfortable so discard them or pass them on to someone who will make better use of them.

ACCESSORIES

Go through scarves, belts and jewellery. Anything broken, unused or that you have multiples of can go. Don't forget to go through any stuff slung on top of a wardrobe or out of sight – when did you last use/wear any of it?

KIDS' CLOTHING

You need to declutter children's clothing fairly regularly as they grow out of items so quickly. I tend to go through Oliver's clothes in the summer and winter because I know he'll have outgrown items once the season comes round again. I'll either keep it, give it away, or if things are really stained, throw it away or take it to my local textile recycling location.

It's sometimes hard to part with special items that bring back memories of your child's younger years, so it helps if you have a meaningful person or place you can pass clothes on to – a family member, friend or favoured charity. You can also sell children's clothes online or at a local event.

ORGANISATION TIPS FOR WARDROBES

Once you've decluttered your wardrobe there are lots of ways you can organise your clothing and accessories. Here are a few ideas:

- Group similar items together. For example, group together trousers, shirts or dresses so you can quickly go through them and choose what to wear.
- Arrange your clothes by colour if that helps you select an outfit, plus it looks great when you open the wardrobe!
- Invest in storage solutions such as baskets, hooks and shoe racks to maximise space and keep items tidy.
- Utilise vertical space – add shelves or hanging organisers on the backs of doors, where you can store shoes, folded clothes or accessories.
- Rotate your clothing seasonally, storing off-season clothes in storage bags to free up space in your wardrobe.
- Place items you use most frequently within easy reach. Reserve higher or out-of-the-way shelves for items that come out less regularly.
- Fold bulkier items, like thick jumpers or jeans.

Living room

Take a critical look at the decorative items in your living room and discard any that you don't like or are damaged. You could even temporarily remove some items, leaving a few statement pieces, to see if that creates a cleaner, calmer (and easier to clean) space.

Go through any DVDs (if you still have any knocking about!), video games and books – are there any you could give away? Remove any dead plants that can't be revived and discard any excess or worn-out cushions. Remove burnt-out candles or used up diffusers. Regularly go through magazines and newspapers and store those you want to keep in a magazine rack or storage box.

Work area

Many of us work from home now, meaning we're bringing more workplace clutter into the home. It can be distracting working in a messy environment, so try to cut down on the clutter on your desk and around you. As well as sorting through and filing all paperwork, chuck any old cables, cords, chargers and tech accessories that you no longer use. Bin any broken or dried-up pens, pencils and stationery, and discard any office freebies that you never use.

Entrance way

This is another area where clutter can build. As it's the first place we enter when coming into our homes, it's where coats are discarded, shoes kicked off and bags put down. Regular five-minute bursts of decluttering will be really effective.

- Go through coats and jackets, especially in different seasons or when the weather changes. These can really pile up if there are multiple people in a household.
- Store seasonal coats you're not using elsewhere (such as individual wardrobes or in storage bags) and donate, recycle or bin any that are damaged or you don't wear any more.
- Sort through hats, gloves and scarves and store any seasonal items.
- Invest in good storage systems, such as hooks, a shoe rack or bench with storage underneath, and an umbrella stand for umbrellas (obviously!) and walking sticks.
- Have a place where you put keys, dog leashes, bags and mail as you come into your home – it might be a key holder, hook, basket or tray. That way you'll know where those items are when you need them.

Bedding

Bedding is another danger spot in our homes. Often we add to our bed linen without discarding older items, making it impossible to find those pillowcases or sheets when we need them. To declutter:

- Collect all your bedding – sheets, pillowcases, duvet covers and blankets – and look through what you have.
- Donate or discard any items that are worn out, that you no longer use or have multiples of. Ideally you should have two sets of bedding per bed.
- Invest in storage, keeping seasonal items, like high tog duvets, in storage bags when not in use.
- Label shelves or storage so you can easily see what's there. You could either store bedding types (e.g. pillowcases, duvet covers) together, or bedding sets

together. A useful hack for the latter is to put the sheets and duvet cover inside a matching pillowcase.

- Store extra blankets or larger pillows close to where you'll need them (such as a blanket box at the end of your bed).

Gift wrap supplies

I love a beautifully wrapped gift, but it's easy for all that ephemera – the wrapping paper, gift bags and boxes, tags, ribbon and tissue paper – to get into a bit of a mess. Here's how to declutter and organise what you have:

- Pull out all your supplies and sort into categories, such as wrapping paper, ribbons and gift bags. Make sure your gift bags are collapsed flat. You may also want to group your supplies according to the occasion, such as Christmas, birthdays or other seasonal celebrations.
- Store items in a laundry hamper, which tend to be tall enough for wrapping paper. Or repurpose a wine carrier for all your bits and pieces. You can even file greeting cards in a labelled concertina file so you can pull out relevant ones when you need them.
- You could devote a wall or corner of a room to gift wrapping, mounting wrapping paper on rolls above a table.

OTHER ITEMS THAT YOU COULD SORT THROUGH AND DECLUTTER IN A FEW MINUTES:

Luggage

Exercise equipment

Hobby related equipment: e.g. fishing, jam-making, knitting, photography

Camping equipment

Christmas or seasonal decorations

Old radios, TVs, phones, computers and other electrical
   devices

Cutlery

Kids' bags

Stationery, pens and pencils

Declutter your life

Why not apply decluttering methods to your life in general. Try
to cut down on anything that takes up your valuable time and
energy so you can focus on what's really important in life. Just
spend five minutes on each task.

- Sort through your phone contacts and delete any
  unwanted ones.
- Remove any unused apps on your phone.
- Go through and delete old and unwanted emails.
- Sort through your photos and have them printed or put
  into a photo book.
- Unsubscribe from blogs and online accounts you no
  longer follow.
- Don't overcommit yourself – say no to invites from time
  to time.
- Remove toxic friends or acquaintances from your life.
- Delete recorded shows and series links on your TV.
- Have some time away from your phone if you can.

Decluttering your home can really help to reduce stress in
your life – you can focus on your work, your family or on watching
TV without that stack of paper screaming at you, and also get
straight down to cleaning without having to clear away mess and
clutter first.

NOTES

CHECKLIST

.... ☐

.... ☐

.... ☐

.... ☐

.... ☐

.... ☐

.... ☐

.... ☐

.... ☐

.... ☐

.... ☐

.... ☐

.... ☐

.... ☐

.... ☐

.... ☐

.... ☐

.... ☐

.... ☐

.... ☐

.... ☐

.... ☐

.... ☐

.... ☐

.... ☐

.... ☐

.... ☐

.... ☐

.... ☐

MONDAY

TUESDAY

WEDNESDAY

THURSDAY

FRIDAY

SATURDAY

SUNDAY

CHAPTER 5

BATHROOM AND TOILET

Bathrooms see a lot of action and, from morning showers to nightly rituals, they can quickly descend into chaos. A room full of steam and splashes also creates the ideal environment for mould, mildew and limescale, and throw a toilet into the mix and you've a hotspot for bacteria and germs. But don't worry, you can keep on top of the mess and moisture with some simple daily habits and just a few minutes of really effective cleaning. Result: a hygienic, fresh and gleaming bathroom.

QUICK CLEANING TIPS

- Do a daily wipe of the sink, toilet and wet surfaces
- Keep cleaning kit close by
- Pick up towels and clothing straightaway
- Put toiletries back after use (with lids on) and bin any that are empty
- Keep your bathroom well ventilated, making sure any extractor fans or vents are working properly
- Keep clutter to a minimum – items on wet surfaces attract mess and mildew
- Make use of mops, squeegees and other time-saving tools

NOTE: many of these tasks are five-minute jobs, but some require soaking an item or applying a product and letting it do its work, and then just a few minutes of hands-on cleaning.

Sink and taps

A bathroom looks instantly better if the sink is clean and the taps are shiny. Give the sink a daily wipe with a cloth or some toilet paper, wiping off any toothpaste, hairs or debris. I use a different face cloth everyday, which I then use to give the sink a quick wipe before putting it in the wash – it takes seconds, I barely think about it, and it makes a visible difference.

On a weekly basis, give the sink and the taps a more thorough clean. I use a scrubbing wand filled with diluted dish soap, scrubbing the inside and outside of the sink, followed by the taps, before wiping dry with a microfibre cloth and buffing up the taps. I might also give the taps and their bases a quick whizz with a sonic scrubber or toothbrush, which will help to remove any build-up of limescale or grime.

If there is limescale on your taps, soak a cloth in white vinegar and wrap it around your taps. Leave for fifteen minutes and then buff with a microfibre glass cloth. Alternatively, pour some white vinegar into a small sandwich bag and tie it on to the tap so the spout is submerged in the vinegar. Leave for about an hour and then scrub away the limescale with a cloth or scrubber.

. . . .

Top tip

If you have any old lemons hanging around, you could cut one in half and press it on to the spout of the tap, tying it on with an elastic band if needed. Leave it for an hour, or longer if possible, to allow the natural acids to do their work, and you should be able to wipe off the limescale.

. . . .

Shower

After you shower, give the screen or wet surfaces a quick squeegee or window vacuum. Removing water residue takes seconds and it's the best way to stop water stains, limescale or mould building up, saving you a lot of bother in the long term. I also keep a scrubbing wand in the shower, and if I put a hair mask or conditioner on my hair, I'll scrub a few surfaces while I'm waiting. (You might as well make the most of your time in the shower, and if you have the kit at hand, why not!)

On a weekly basis, wipe down the tiles, shower tray, controls and screen. For speed I use a spin mop as the head can easily manoeuvre around the curves. I fill its bucket with warm water and a squirt of dish soap, then mop and dry with a squeegee or window vacuum, buffing any streaks with a microfibre glass cloth.

If water stains or limescale have built up on your shower screen, squirt some white vinegar or Viakal on to it, let it sit for a few minutes and then clean with a power scrubber, scrubbing wand or the abrasive side of a Minky bathroom cloth. Dry with a squeegee, window vacuum or glass cloth.

Fact check

What is limescale?

When water evaporates, it leaves behind calcium and magnesium deposits, called limescale. Hard water has a higher mineral content so will leave behind more deposits, but over time soft water can leave deposits too.

What is mould and mildew?

These are types of fungi that thrive in damp, warm places and can often be seen on wet surfaces in bathrooms. Mould is darker in colour and can penetrate surfaces, while mildew is lighter in colour and easier to wipe away. Both are unhealthy, especially for people with allergies or asthma.

Shower head

Aim to descale your shower head around once a month. An easy way to do this is to place the head in a bowl or sink filled with white vinegar and leave it to soak for thirty minutes to an hour. Scrub with an old toothbrush or sonic scrubber to remove the limescale. Repeat if necessary. If your shower head doesn't unscrew, tie a food bag filled with white vinegar around your shower head.

NOTE: do not use this method if your shower head is nickel-coated, and if it is made from brass do not soak for longer than thirty minutes as it could ruin the finish.

Shower hose

The same method applies to the shower hose. Detach it and sit it in a bowl of vinegar for thirty minutes to an hour, depending on what it is made of. If there is still some gunk in the grooves, scrub with a toothbrush or sonic scrubber.

Shower curtain

Bacteria and mould can build quickly on a shower curtain so you should clean it monthly, or at least every two months. Remove it and put in a washing machine with detergent and 120 ml (½ cup) white vinegar. Wash in cold water if plastic or vinyl, and warm water if fabric, but always check the care label first. You could also add a few drops of tea tree oil to the white vinegar to prevent the build-up of mould.

Bath

Rinse out the bath after each use and dry any ledges or tiles around it with a dry microfibre cloth or towel, to prevent mould growth.

Clean the bath and surrounding surfaces every week, including the outside of the bath, with diluted dish soap. It's quick and easy to use a spin mop to do this. If the taps need attention, spray them with vinegar and clean with a scrubbing wand or follow the instructions above for sink taps (see page 126).

If the bath is particular grimy with soap scum (see Tip below), spray it with white vinegar, let it sit for a few minutes, then mop it and rinse thoroughly. Dry any surrounding ledges or tiles.

NOTE: if you have an enamel bath, it's best to use only a mild detergent and avoid any strong acidic cleaning products or abrasive scourers.

Top tip

If you run your hand down the inside of the bath, you can feel if there is any soap scum (a filmy layer of soap and mineral residue) – a clean bath should be smooth; a layer of soap scum will feel a little rougher.

Tile grouting

Remove and prevent mould by mixing 270 g (1 cup) bicarbonate of soda, 240 ml (1 cup) hydrogen peroxide, 240 ml (1 cup) dish soap and a few drops of tea tree oil. Apply to the grouting with a toothbrush or cloth. Let it sit for around twenty minutes and then scrub away with a sonic scrubber or toothbrush.

Mould and mildew

To remove any mould or mildew on tile grouting, bath or shower ledges or seals, spray on a DIY spray made up of 240 ml (1 cup) white vinegar and 30–40 drops of tea tree oil and leave for ten to fifteen minutes, then rinse and wipe.

Let's go over how you can give your bathroom a thorough clean over a seven-day period.

Monday – deep-clean toilet and disinfect toilet brush
Tuesday – clean shower/screen or bath and surrounding tiles/surfaces

Wednesday – clean sink, taps and mirrors
Thursday – mop floor and walls
Friday – wash towels, mats and shower curtain
Saturday – flush out plug holes, wipe cupboards and
   surfaces
Sunday – disinfect toothbrush, empty and wipe bins

Plug holes

Clean your plug holes regularly, at least once a month, to prevent a build-up of grime, hair and soap that can lead to blockages.

First clean out any hair or gunk with a paper towel, twisting it one end and putting it into the plug hole while holding on to the other end. You could also use a long drain-cleaning brush which has hooks on it to pull out any hair or debris – you'll be amazed what comes out! Alternatively, you can use a traditional plunger to dislodge or bring any gunk up to the surface.

Then pour down 270 g (1 cup) bicarbonate of soda and 480 ml (2 cups) white vinegar. Hold a cloth over the plug hole for a minute or two to force the reaction downwards. Then pour boiling water down the hole and add a few drops of tea tree or lemon essential oil to get rid of any odour.

Toilet

Cleaning the toilet may not be everyone's favourite job, but it's a vital one if you want a hygienic and fresh-smelling bathroom. Toilets host huge amounts of bacteria, viruses and unpleasant stenches, but the right techniques and products, plus just five minutes of cleaning, will keep your toilet sparkling and germ-free!

If your toilet sees a lot of use you might need to give it a good clean every day, but at least once or twice a week is recommended. If you want to avoid bleach or harsh chemicals, citric acid or soda crystals are a good natural option for the toilet bowl, and a DIY all-purpose cleaner (see page 35) for the cistern.

. . . .

Deep-clean

The following instructions are for a deep-clean of the toilet using citric acid, which should remove any water stains at the bottom.

Gloves
Hot water
Citric acid
DIY all-purpose cleaner (see page 35)
Paper towels
Toilet brush

Put on some gloves and pour hot or just-boiled water down the toilet. Sprinkle in 200 g (½ cup) citric acid. Let it fizz for five minutes.

In the meantime, spray the cistern with all-purpose cleaner, working from the top to the bottom, spraying the lid and seat and their undersides, around the hinges, then all around the top of the bowl, under the rim, and down the sides of the toilet to the base. Leave to sit for two minutes.

Then, with a paper towel, wipe down the outside of the toilet from the top to the lid, seat and base. Use a toothbrush or sonic scrubber to deal with any grime around the seat hinges.

Give the bowl a scrub with the toilet brush, including all around the top, rim and down to the bottom. Flush the toilet, rinsing through the toilet brush, and place the brush between the seat and toilet bowl, brush end over the bowl, to dry.

The above should be done once or twice a week, depending on how much the toilet is used.

Daily clean

To keep your toilet fresh on a daily basis, sprinkle in some citric acid and scrub with the brush. Leave for a couple of hours then flush. Do this when you know it won't be in use for a while – perhaps before you go to work or take the kids to school.

Steam clean

Steam cleaning is also a quick and easy way to clean a toilet, particularly because the heat will eliminate germs and loosen stains. Direct all over the toilet, including around the hinges, and attach a brush attachment to scrub any stains in the bowl. Use a paper towel to wipe up any grime, and a microfibre cloth to dry any moisture on the toilet exterior. For a scent boost you could add a few drops of fresh-smelling essential oil to the water in your steam cleaner.

Toilet brush

It's a good idea to disinfect your toilet brush every month. Spray it with disinfectant, then place between the seat and toilet bowl, brush end over the bowl, and air-dry for thirty minutes to two hours. Also remember to spray the toilet brush container, let that sit for at least a couple of minutes and wipe dry with a paper towel.

Top tips

- To remove limescale on the
toilet bowl, gently scrub with a
pumice stick (it's best if the
pumice stone and toilet are wet to
avoid scratching the porcelain). After
use, spray the pumice with a DIY disinfectant
spray (see page 42), allow it to air-dry and keep in
a zip-lock bag.

- To remove unsightly water stains and limescale build-up at the bottom of the bowl, an overnight treatment might be required. Remove the water, either with a cup or by soaking it up in an old cloth. Pour in a lime-scale remover product – either white vinegar or a chemical-based product, depending on your preference – and leave overnight. Then scrub with the toilet brush and flush to wash away any deposits.

- To whiten your toilet bowl if it looks discoloured or stained, drop in one or two denture tablets and let them sit in the water for an hour or two. Use your brush to scrub away any stains, then flush. You could do this on a monthly basis.

- The floor around a toilet can sometimes develop a bad aroma (we're talking a urine odour). What can get rid of the smell? Shaving foam! A cheap one will work just as well, so apply a generous layer of foam to the area, leave for ten to thirty minutes, then mop or wipe off. You can then also spray on a disinfectant allowing it to dry.

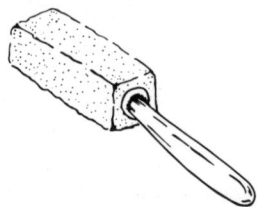

QUICK FIVE-MINUTE CLEANS

The following three jobs could take five minutes in total.

1. Mirrors

Clean with a scrubbing wand filled with dish soap and water – I often do this after cleaning my sink and shower screen – or you could spray on some white vinegar and then buff dry with a glass microfibre cloth, using small circular motions.

2. Bins

Wipe the outside, and if chrome buff up to a shine with a damp microfibre cloth. Empty your bins weekly and, to keep them smelling fresh, add a cotton wool ball dampened with a few drops of essential oil.

3. Toothbrush

Rinse your toothbrush every day with warm water and leave to air dry. Ideally you should disinfect your tooth-brush once a week. You can do this either by putting it in boiling water for two to three minutes or by filling a cup with antibacterial mouthwash or cool water and half a denture tablet. Soak the brush for around two minutes and rinse well.

Bonus tips

- Invest in a new toothbrush or toothbrush head every three months, and keep your toothbrush covered or in a cabinet, well away from the toilet.

- When flushing your toilet after use, it's best to do it with the lid closed. One flush can produce thousands of tiny aerosol droplets containing bacteria and viruses, which can contaminate surfaces (and your toothbrush) up to six feet away!

- Does your mirror fog up? Shaving foam will stop that happening! Simply apply a small squirt of shaving foam to the mirror, and then wipe and buff dry with a clean microfibre cloth. The anti-fog protection will last for a few days to a few weeks.

- Put a pot of bicarbonate of soda on a ledge or surface in your bathroom – this will help to absorb any odours. Change every couple of weeks.

Cupboards and surfaces

Wipe down the outside doors of cupboards, the handles and on top where dust accumulates. You can use a scrubbing wand, spin mop or microfibre cloth. Every month or so, take out your toiletries and cupboard items, decluttering as you go, and wipe down the insides with a multi-purpose cleaner. In five minutes, you can tackle one shelf at a time or types of items, such as sorting through suncreams or face cloths.

Wipe surfaces and ledges, and any items on them. Water

plants and dust their leaves with a damp cloth or old make-up brush.

Walls

To dust the walls and any skirting boards, a Flash Speed Mop with dust magnet pads is ideal. Then clean with a flat-headed mop.

Floors

Vacuum or sweep, then clean using a spin or flat-headed mop and soapy water, adding tea tree or a citrus essential oil for a fresh-smelling scent.

Chrome radiators

Remove any debris or dust with a microfibre cloth. Spray with the DIY glass cleaner (see page 35) and wipe dry with a microfibre cloth.

Over time, rust can sometimes appear on a chrome radiator. To remove it, dampen a cloth with white vinegar and rub on to the affected area. You could also try rubbing the area with dampened aluminium foil – the resulting chemical reaction can remove the rust. Give the chrome another final buff up with a clean side of the cloth, and for extra shine you could buff with a few drops of baby oil.

Extractor fan/vent

Extractor fans and vents help to remove odours and moisture, preventing the build up of mould and mildew, and improve the air quality in bathrooms. As a result, it's in your interest to ensure they're working well and to give them a good clean from time to time. The covers tend to attract dust, so use a static duster; they're often high up so you need something with a long arm.

To clean the fan or vent itself, you'll need to remove the cover. To do so safely, switch off the power supply. Remove the cover and place it in a container of soapy water. Take a look at the fan and vent and, if needed, dust it with a vacuum nozzle or duster, or wipe off any dirt with a toothbrush. Wipe and dry the covers and put back on.

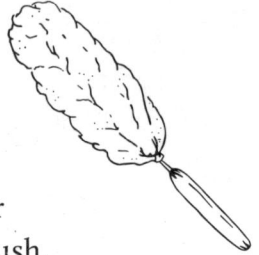

Bathroom light switch or cord

They're often overlooked, but light switches and cords can harbour lots of bacteria and germs. Spray with the DIY all-purpose cleaner or disinfectant (see pages 35 and 42). If the cord needs whitening, mix together a paste of bicarbonate of soda and white vinegar and apply. Leave for ten minutes and rinse off.

Toothbrush holders

Don't forget to wash your toothbrush holder. Soak it in a solution of dish soap and vinegar, then rinse and air-dry.

Bath towels

Bath towels should be washed after three uses. A hot 60°C (140°F) temperature is better at killing germs. Use your normal detergent but avoid fabric softener as it can create a build-up on the fibres over time, causing them to feel rough to the touch, and it can also irritate sensitive skin.

Bathmats

These should be washed weekly. To remove any odour, sprinkle them with bicarbonate of soda and leave for at least thirty minutes before washing. Then wash with your usual detergent and 120 ml (½ cup) white vinegar.

BATHROOM CHECKLIST

DAILY

> Wipe the sink
> Squeegee/window vacuum shower screen and tiles
> Rinse out bath and dry ledges/tiles
> Add toilet cleaner and give it a quick scrub
> Rinse toothbrush
> Pick up clothes and towels
> Put away toiletries

WEEKLY

> Clean the sinks and taps
> Deep-clean the toilet
> Mop the shower tiles, tray and screen
> Clean the bath and surrounding surfaces
> Disinfect the toilet brush
> Clean mirrors
> Empty bins
> Wipe surfaces, ledges and cupboards
> Dust and mop walls

Vacuum/sweep floors, then mop
Dust and clean chrome radiators
Disinfect toothbrush
Wash bath towels and mats

MONTHLY

Remove any build-up/limescale on shower screen
Wash shower curtain
Clean plug holes
Whiten toilet bowl
Declutter toiletries
Clean and disinfect bathroom light or switch

SEASONAL

Clean and whiten tile grouting
Descale shower head and hose
Remove any mould or mildew
Remove any rust on radiators
Clean extractor fan or vent

NOTES

....

....

....

....

....

....

....

....

....

....

....

CHECKLIST

- .... ☐
- .... ☐
- .... ☐
- .... ☐
- .... ☐
- .... ☐
- .... ☐
- .... ☐
- .... ☐
- .... ☐
- .... ☐
- .... ☐

BATHROOM AND TOILET

.... ☐

.... ☐

.... ☐

.... ☐

.... ☐

.... ☐

.... ☐

.... ☐

.... ☐

.... ☐

.... ☐

.... ☐

.... ☐

.... ☐

.... ☐

.... ☐

.... ☐

MONDAY

TUESDAY

WEDNESDAY

THURSDAY

FRIDAY

SATURDAY

SUNDAY

CHAPTER 6

KITCHEN

The kitchen is often seen as the heart of the home, a bustling hub where meals are prepared and shared with families and friends. With frequent food spills, cooking odours and mess that can accumulate in minutes, it's easy to be overwhelmed trying to keep on top of the kitchen. But you can maintain a clean and hygienic kitchen by giving it a quick daily reset and clean by using the right tools and products, and by following the Five-Minute Clean Routine!

QUICK CLEANING TIPS

- Clean as you go – wipe worktops and hob after use, clean up spillages immediately, and wipe down the sink daily
- Wash and put away dishes every day
- Make use of effective tools – spray mops, extendable power scrubbers and window vacuums speed up cleaning on large surface areas
- Ask household members to help
- Declutter regularly
- Make sure your cooker hood and filters are clean and working

Worktops

Wipe down kitchen worktops on a daily basis, removing any crumbs and spills with a mild dish soap and water solution. You can spray a DIY all-purpose or disinfectant cleaner (see pages 35 and 42), let it sit for a few minutes, then wipe clean with a microfibre cloth or dry with a window vacuum. For speed you can also use a steam cleaner, but do avoid using on anything containing electrical components and keep away from power sockets.

To give the worktops a more thorough clean, remove any items and wipe the whole surface. The best method for cleaning depends on your type of worktop, as some materials are more durable than others. Abrasive cleaning products or scourers, for example, can damage laminate or stainless-steel surfaces, as can anything acidic or containing bleach on a granite, marble or quartz worktop. Some stains, including tea and coffee spills, can be removed by applying a paste of bicarbonate of soda and water, letting it sit for a few minutes and scrubbing gently with a soft brush or cloth, but test on an inconspicuous area before use. Steam cleaners should not be used on wooden worktops as the excess moisture can damage the surface.

To remove finger marks and restore shine on a stainless-steel worktop, use a microfibre glass cloth or apply a small amount of baby oil or olive oil and buff the surface. Wooden worktops might require oiling every few months to restore shine and to protect the natural grain of the wood.

Sinks

Rinse your sink after every use – I use a Scrub Daddy scrubbing wand and dish soap. For a more thorough clean, and if your sink is a little discoloured, sprinkle in some bicarbonate of soda and a squirt of dish soap, scrub with a wet sponge, scrubbing wand or power scrubber, and rinse. If you have a stainless-steel sink, you can apply a little baby oil and buff dry with a dry microfibre cloth for extra shine.

To whiten an enamel or porcelain sink, fill your sink with water, add a couple of denture tablets and soak for twenty minutes. Then drain the water, rinse and wipe with a dry cloth.

Taps

Give your taps a quick wipe every day with a cloth, scrubbing wand, or whichever tool you're using on your sinks or worktops.

To remove any limescale on your taps, soak a paper towel or an absorbent cloth in white vinegar and tie it securely around the tap using elastic bands, or cover it with a food bag. Leave for a few hours, or overnight, and you should be able to scrub away the limescale with an old toothbrush.

Drains

Flush out your drains using 270 g (1 cup) bicarbonate of soda and 480 ml (2 cups) white vinegar. Cover the plug hole with a cloth for three to four minutes to keep the reaction travelling down the drain, dislodging any blockages. Rinse with hot water and a capful of disinfectant. Soda crystals are another great product to use – just dissolve 200 g (1 cup) of soda crystals in 500 ml– 1 litre (1–2 pints) boiling water and carefully pour down the drain. Pour more boiling water down the drain to clear everything.

. . . .

Top tip

Avoid putting cooking oil or grease down your drain, as fat solidifies and is the most common cause of blocked drains. Instead, line your drain cover with tin foil to make a shallow bowl and carefully pour the cooled fats into it before discarding.

. . . .

Hob

A clean hob or stove top can change the look of a kitchen, but just one cooking session can result in greasy splatters everywhere. For that reason, it's best to clean your hob every day, or at least after every use, wiping up any food or liquid spillages with a paper towel.

To clean my glass induction hob, I use a scrubbing wand with a little dish soap and warm water, then wipe down and dry with a microfibre cloth. To clean the hob more thoroughly, make a paste of bicarbonate of soda and warm water (creating a slightly thinner consistency than toothpaste) and scrub with a sponge. Test the paste on an inconspicuous area first to check the bicarbonate of soda doesn't scratch the surface.

I also regularly use my steam cleaner on the hob, focusing on the edges, loosening or softening any grime that has accumulated there. You could also use a cocktail stick wrapped in a paper towel or a knife wrapped in a microfibre cloth, running it around the edge to collect any grime. To shine up my hob, I give it a buff with a microfibre cloth. I like my Marigold Squeaky Clean Flexi Microfibre Cloth, which you could use on other shiny surfaces in the kitchen, from fridges and tiles to worktops. For stainless-steel hobs, you can also apply baby oil with a cloth for a streak-free shine.

Splashbacks

The quickest method for cleaning splashbacks is to use a scrubbing wand or power scrubber with dish soap to remove grease or dirt. You could also use a steam cleaner, particularly if your splashback is tiled, using the grout cleaning method (see page 130) if the grouting is discoloured. For a glass splashback, use an all-purpose glass spray, or apply rubbing alcohol, and wipe down with a cloth or window vacuum.

Cupboards

Finger marks, grease and grime can build up on cupboard doors, so I wipe these down using warm soapy water and an extendable power scrubber – it's quicker than using a cloth, can clean large, high-up areas and does the scrubbing for you! If you have glass-fronted cabinets, I recommend adding a splash of white vinegar to your soapy water, or use a DIY glass spray (see page 35) to keep them streak-free.

When doing a more thorough clean it's best to work top to bottom, so when I do my cabinets, I work downwards with my power scrubber, finishing with the baseboards, which can often get scuffed and dirty. (Depending on the style of your kitchen, you could do the baseboards when cleaning the floor, using a flat-headed mop.)

On a monthly or seasonal basis, clean out your cupboards by removing items, decluttering as you go, and wiping down the insides with hot soapy water. Dry with a cloth or air-dry and return the items. In five minutes, you can tackle a shelf at a time – just remember to begin at the top of the cupboard and work down.

Floors

Sweep or vacuum your floors on a daily basis – food and debris can accumulate quickly, and it's a job that can be done in a just a minute or two. For speed, I mop the kitchen floor with a spray mop, using just dish soap and water. I also vacuum or shake out my floor mats regularly.

Walls

I give the walls and ceiling a dust and clean every few months, working top to bottom. I use my static duster or

Flash mop with duster pads, then mop the walls with my flat-headed mop.

Light fixtures

I dust the light fixtures monthly and clean them every few months. I have glass pendant lights in my kitchen so I'll take them down, rinse the glass in hot soapy water, let them air-dry, then buff with my Marigold Squeaky Clean Flexi Microfibre Cloth. (Incidentally, when I dust my light fixtures, I often check the smoke alarm as well as it's located nearby – it's recommended you do this weekly or at least once a month.)

Let's go over how you can give your kitchen a thorough clean over a seven-day period.

Monday – clean sink, taps and hob
Tuesday – mop floor, wipe down tiles and splashbacks
Wednesday – clean and declutter fridge
Thursday – clean windows
Friday – descale kettle, clean chopping board and microwave
Saturday – flush out plug holes, clean bins and declutter one cupboard
Sunday – give pots and pans a deep-clean, clean coffee machine or toaster

Fridge

Fridges are in constant use and a key part of the kitchen. Declutter them regularly, chucking out anything that has passed its expiry date or you haven't used for months. Clean up any spillages or leaks immediately and give the handle a daily wipe with warm soapy water.

On a weekly basis, wipe down the surfaces inside with warm soapy water and dry with a cloth. Do the same on the outside, removing any grubby finger marks, and if you have a stainless-steel fridge, buff the outside using a microfibre glass cloth with olive or baby oil or rubbing alcohol.

I also like to clean the fridge using a steam cleaner, which, with the right nozzle, can really get into all the crevices. If you don't have a steam cleaner, use a cocktail stick wrapped in tissue to remove grime from crevices and edges.

On a monthly or seasonal basis, remove all the items from the fridge, including the shelves and drawers. Give them a wash in warm soapy water – you could put them in the dishwasher, although you should allow them to come to room temperature first – wipe dry and put everything back. Wipe over the insides with a soft, damp cloth dipped in bicarbonate of soda before wiping over again with a cloth rinsed in warm soapy water. This job will take more than five minutes, so tackle it only when you have the time or motivation, or clean in five-minute chunks, focusing on one shelf or vegetable drawer at a time.

Top tip

Keep a small pot of bicarbonate of soda in the fridge to absorb any odours. Replace it every couple of weeks.

Bins

A bin spilling over with rubbish is never a pretty sight and the key culprit of odours in the kitchen. Empty when needed and give your bin a wipe, inside and out, at least once a week with antibacterial spray. If you're cleaning a big bin, you could use a flat-headed or spray mop for speed. Dry with a cloth or allow to air-dry and, to keep odours at bay, add 540 g (2 cups) bicarbonate of soda and 5 drops of essential oil to the base before adding your bin bag.

QUICK FIVE-MINUTE CLEANS

Here are some quick five-minute cleans for various bits of equipment around the kitchen.

1. Chopping board

With everyday use, wooden chopping boards can develop little cuts and grooves where bacteria can lurk, so it's important to clean them properly. Wash your chopping board in hot soapy water after every use but don't soak it in water for more than a few minutes and don't put it in the dishwasher. Once a month it's a good idea to give it a thorough clean, to keep it germ-free as well as remove any stains or odours. Sprinkle the board with bicarbonate of soda or salt, then rub half a lemon all over, scrubbing in small circles. Let that sit for five minutes, then rinse everything off and air-dry completely before using.

2. Toaster

Switch off the power, then remove the trays, discard the crumbs and wipe down the trays. Use a hair dryer to blast out any trapped crumbs, positioning it downwards towards the base of the toaster. Wipe down the outside of the toaster with DIY kitchen cleaner (see page 35). Any burn marks on the top can be removed by scrubbing with a paste of bicarbonate of soda and warm water or a magic eraser.

3. Blender or food processor

This couldn't be simpler. Disconnect the blender/food processor from the power source and wipe down the base and cord with a damp cloth. Fill the container or jug halfway with hot water from the tap, add a few drops of dish soap, put the lid on, and give it a whizz for thirty seconds. Pour the contents into the sink, rinse the container or jug and lid, and allow to air-dry. If you do this every time you use your blender, you shouldn't need to scrub or deep-clean it.

4. Mugs

To remove mug stains, fill them halfway with boiling water, add white vinegar, allow to sit for five minutes, then scrub. Rinse out when done. Alternatively, mix a little bicarbonate of soda and some water into a paste, scrub with a sponge and rinse thoroughly.

5. Coffee machine

Like kettles, coffee machines work better after a good clean, plus your coffee will taste better if you clean out any residue. If you have a drip coffee maker, wash the carafe and filter basket every day with warm soapy water and rinse thoroughly. On a monthly basis, fill the water reservoir with equal parts water and white vinegar and run a brewing cycle without coffee grounds. This will help descale the internal components and prevent mineral build-up. Then run at least two cycles with just water to clean out any vinegar residue.

For a single-serve pod coffee maker, remove the water reservoir, drip tray and any other removable components and wash in warm soapy water, then rinse thoroughly. You should also run the descaling cycle recommended by the manufacturer. For an espresso machine, refer to the manufacturer's instructions for cleaning and maintenance.

Top tip

If your scissors are blunt, cutting aluminium foil will sharpen them. It really does work!

Microwave

To avoid any build-up of odour or food residue, wipe the plate and the insides of the microwave after each use. For a more thorough clean, add a slice of lemon to a bowl of water and microwave for three minutes. Leave to stand for five minutes before removing and wiping down your microwave. The lemon steam will clean and cut through any grease and grime that's built up.

Air fryer

Sprinkle 135 g (½ cup) bicarbonate of soda and a little dish soap on to the trays. Fill halfway with boiling water and let it sit for at least thirty minutes. This will break down any grease. Pour out the liquid, then scrub with some more dish soap, rinse and air-dry.

Descale the kettle

This is one of those pleasing tasks because (a) nobody wants scaly bits floating in their tea and (b) any build-up of limescale can cause your kettle to be less efficient or even burn out. To prevent this, descale your kettle once a month by combining 1 tablespoon of citric acid with enough water to cover the bottom of your kettle. Bring it to the boil and let it sit for twenty minutes before emptying out the mixture. Finally, rinse thoroughly with fresh water.

Cutlery

To remove stains on stainless-steel cutlery, mix one part white vinegar to eight parts hot water in a washing-up bowl. Add your cutlery and leave for five to ten minutes. Rinse clean and dry with a cloth.

Pots, pans and baking trays

It's always best to soak or wash pots and pans straight after use in hot soapy water as debris will come off more easily.

When it comes to stubborn, burnt-on food or stains, bicarbonate of soda is your best friend. It works well with most types of pans, including stainless-steel, cast-iron, ceramic and the outside of non-stick pans. Sprinkle bicarbonate of soda over the stain, add a little water and dish soap, and scrub. For more resistant stains, you could add 240 ml (1 cup) water, about a tablespoon of bicarbonate of soda, 120 ml (½ cup) white vinegar and then boil on the hob for ten minutes. The food or stain should wipe away easily, and then rinse.

To remove scorch marks on the underside of pans, apply a paste made of three parts bicarbonate of soda to one part warm water. Let it sit for about ten minutes, then scrub with a sponge and most of the marks should come off. For a bit more oomph you could add a little dish soap to the paste or add some vinegar while scrubbing.

A dilute paste of bicarbonate of soda and water should be

safe to use on most non-stick cookware, but check the manufacturer's instructions and don't scrub your non-stick pans with anything abrasive, such as a scourer or wire wool, which could damage the coating. If you want to avoid using bicarbonate of soda, fill the pan or tray with water, add 120 ml (½ cup) white vinegar, bring to the boil, and any residue or burnt-on food should float to the top. Pour out and wash in soapy water.

Glasses

Wash glasses in hot soapy water and, when washing up by hand, always do your glasses first. Rinse straightway and leave to air-dry, or dry with a microfibre cloth or paper towel.

To remove hard water stains or cloudiness, you could add white vinegar to soapy washing-up water or spray on some of your DIY glass spray (see page 35), then rinse off with warm water and dry immediately with a microfibre cloth or paper towel. In a dishwasher, put 240 ml (1 cup) vinegar in the top rack. If there is a particularly stubborn water stain you could also try crumpling up an old newspaper, dampening it with your DIY glass spray, and then scrubbing the stain before washing off.

....

Top tip

Some people also swear by scrunching up a ball of aluminium foil and placing it in the dishwasher during a wash cycle. Result: sparkling glasses, crockery and cutlery!

....

CORRECT ORDER FOR WASHING UP BY HAND

1. Glasses
2. Lightly soiled items
3. Cups and mugs
4. Plates (food scraped and rinsed off)
5. Cutlery
6. Cooking dishes and pans

Dishwasher

I can't quite imagine life without my dishwasher – I use it every day and it's a real time-saver. As it's also a big investment, I'm keen to keep it in good working order, and there are a few easy things you can do to help with this.

Get into the habit of scraping off as much food residue as you can from pots and pans. If you've eaten something like porridge, which can harden like cement if left to dry, then soak the pan and bowl before putting in the dishwasher.

Make sure the dishwater salt is topped up. Salt stops the build-up of hard water deposits and helps to keep the dishwasher clean by preventing bacteria build-up.

Rinse out the filter once a week. Remove it, rinse it under a tap to dislodge anything, leave to dry and put it back in.

Every two to three months, give the inside door, sides and seals a scrub with soapy water, then place a cup of white vinegar in the top rack and put on a hot cycle. To deodorise the machine, you can also sprinkle a couple of tablespoons of bicarbonate of soda in the bottom, leave for at least fifteen minutes, then run a hot cycle. Result: a dishwasher that's as good as new!

```
........................................................
```

HOW TO LOAD A DISHWASHER

- Load large items along the sides and the back so they don't block water and detergent.
- Place items with burnt-on food in the bottom rack, face down towards the sprays.
- Place glasses and mugs upside down so they don't fill with water.
- Place delicate (but dishwasher-safe) items on the top rack.
- Load forks together, knives together etc., so they can be quickly unloaded.
- Check the dishwasher manual because it will also advise on loading, temperatures and the correct cycles to run.

```
........................................................
```

Do not put the following in a dishwasher: wooden items, crystal or delicate glassware, plastic not labelled dishwasher-safe, kitchen knives or blades (as high heat can dull them), non-stick pans, cast-iron or aluminium baking trays, copper, aluminium or cast-iron pots and pans, insulated coffee or water mugs.

Surprising things you can put in the dishwasher to save time

- Oven shelves and liners
- Microwave turntable
- Fridge shelves (that don't have integrated LED lights) – allow them to come to room temperature before putting in the dishwasher to avoid cracks
- Children's plastic toys, teethers, dummies (put them in a laundry mesh bag)

- Plastic combs and hairbrushes
- Hair accessories
- Toothbrush holders
- Soap trays
- Exhaust fan covers and filters
- Cleaning brushes
- Squeegees
- Dustpan and brush

Deep-cleaning jobs

Over time, items in the kitchen need a thorough clean. These tend to be bigger jobs but some are less time-consuming than you might think and mini daily cleans will also make these jobs much easier.

Electric or gas hob

There are lots of different types of hob or stove top, so refer to the user manual for cleaning and maintenance tips, or try out a product or tool on a small inconspicuous area first.

Before cleaning, switch off the power and make sure the hob is cold. For an electric stove top with burners (also known as coils or rings), wipe away any dirt or spills with a cloth dampened with soapy water. For any stubborn grime, make a cleaning paste with bicarbonate of soda and water, rub it on and leave it to sit for twenty minutes. Wipe up the paste and let the hob dry completely before using.

If you have a gas hob with racks and burners, take the cooled racks off and soak them in hot soapy water. If they aren't coated you could use a scouring pad to scrub off stubborn stains, or if coated use a sponge. Burner caps can be cleaned in the same way as the gas rings, using a sponge or an old toothbrush to get into all the grooves. Rinse off with cold water and allow to air-dry. Clean the hob, removing all food residue and stains, being careful not to damage the burners, and then carefully put everything back into position on the hob.

For induction hobs, see page 150.

Cooker hood

Your cooker hood helps to prevent grease settling on kitchen surfaces and reduces unpleasant odours, so it's important to keep it clean and clog-free. If there is an aluminium mesh filter, you can usually remove it and wash it in hot soapy water with a sponge or put it in the dishwasher. Rinse thoroughly and pat dry. If you have a paper filter, replace it if it is saturated with grease – they should be changed every three months to a year, depending on how much you cook.

To clean the metal hood, make a paste using one part bicarbonate of soda and one part white vinegar, then rub the paste on to the hood, going with the grain of the metal. (Use a microfibre cloth or sponge; don't use a scourer or anything too abrasive as it can scratch the metal.) Cooker hoods can get quite grimy, so you might need to employ a bit of elbow grease! Take care if you're having to reach up high. Once finished, wipe away the residue with a damp cloth.

Oven

It's recommended to clean your oven every three to six months. So if you're in the mood or you have some time to spare, then go for it! If not, there's no shame in getting someone in to help and paying for a professional oven clean.

1. Remove the shelves and sweep out the bottom of the oven with a dry cloth.
2. Add 270–540 g (1–2 cups) bicarbonate of soda to a bowl and make a paste by adding a few drops of warm water (the consistency should be slightly thinner than toothpaste).
3. Put on rubber gloves and apply a generous layer of the paste to the base, sides and inside of the door, as well as the shelves. These can be placed back into the oven now.
4. Leave for a couple of hours, then take the shelves back out and place in the sink. Wipe away the excess paste from the oven with a damp, warm cloth. An oven scraper can be used for any tough, burnt-on food.
5. Finally, wipe away excess paste from the shelves with a damp, warm cloth. A scourer can be used if needed.
6. Replace the shelves and wipe the front of the oven with warm soapy water or a disinfectant spray and microfibre cloth.

. . . .

Top tip

If your oven shelves are particularly grimy or covered in burnt-on food, put them outside on the grass overnight and any food residue or stains will easily wipe off. Alternatively, soak them overnight in a sink filled with very hot water and 3–4 large scoops of bicarbonate of soda. You can clean barbecue grill racks in the same way.

. . . .

Freezer

Thankfully, many modern freezers come with a frost-free feature so you shouldn't need to defrost them as often as you did in the past. If ice build-up becomes noticeable, however, you will need to defrost your freezer, the upside of which is that it will give you the opportunity to clean it and sort through items inside.

To defrost a freezer, you need to switch it off and remove all the items. Chuck anything that's past its expiry date or is just taking up room and never likely to be used. Place newspaper around the freezer to soak up any water, and towels inside the freezer to soak up melting ice. Remove the shelves and drawers – you may need to wait until the ice has thawed to do this – and give them a wash in soapy water then dry with a cloth. When all the ice has thawed, wash the insides with soapy water and dry as much as you can to prevent ice forming immediately. Switch the freezer back on, and give it time to cool down before putting frozen food back in.

Windows

Kitchen windows often need more regular cleaning than elsewhere in the home. The good news is that it can take just a few minutes to clean a window, especially if you have a squeegee or window vacuum. Here's how:

1. Fill a bucket with 3.75 litres (1 gallon) warm water, 60 ml (¼ cup) dish soap and 60 ml (¼ cup) white vinegar.
2. Scrub the windows with a flat-headed mop.
3. Remove the suds and dry using a window vacuum or squeegee.

To clean the window frames and sills, dust them with a cloth or static duster, then wipe them with soapy water, using a sonic scrubber or toothbrush to get into crevices and hinges. For sliding window tracks, remove any dust using a small brush specially made for tracks. If you don't have a brush, use a vacuum nozzle, with the inside of a toilet roll wedged over the end and pinched in to make the opening narrower.

. . . .

Top tip

When vacuuming or squeegeeing the windows, use the 'S' technique instead of the usual circular motion. When cleaning any surface, the 'S' action is more effective because it avoids going over the same area twice as you would if cleaning in circles. Put your squeegee near the top of the windowpane and glide it down using an 'S' motion from the top to the bottom. Repeat until you've squeegeed the whole window.

. . . .

KITCHEN CHECKLIST

DAILY

Wipe down or steam kitchen worktops and hob
Rinse out sink
Wash and put away dishes
Sweep or vacuum floor
Empty bin if needed
Change dishcloth used to wipe surfaces

WEEKLY

Give the sink and taps a thorough clean
Whiten an enamel sink or buff up a stainless-steel sink

Wipe down tiles and splashbacks
Mop the kitchen floor
Wipe down inside surfaces of fridge
Wipe down bins
Rinse out dishwasher filter

MONTHLY

Flush out drains
Wipe outside of cupboards
Remove fridge items and clean shelves, drawers and insides
Give chopping board a thorough clean
Descale kettle
Clean out toaster
Clean microwave
Clean coffee machine
Gives pots, pans and baking trays a thorough clean
Clean windows
Test smoke alarm

SEASONAL

Clean inside of cupboards and declutter
Mop walls and light fixtures
Remove stains on cutlery
Clean blender or food mixer
Remove mug stains
Deep-clean dishwasher
Deep-clean electric or gas hob
Clean cooker hood
Clean oven
Clean window frames and runners

NOTES

CHECKLIST

- [ ] ....
- [ ] ....
- [ ] ....
- [ ] ....
- [ ] ....
- [ ] ....
- [ ] ....
- [ ] ....
- [ ] ....
- [ ] ....
- [ ] ....
- [ ] ....

KITCHEN

.... ☐

.... ☐

.... ☐

.... ☐

.... ☐

.... ☐

.... ☐

.... ☐

.... ☐

.... ☐

.... ☐

.... ☐

.... ☐

.... ☐

.... ☐

.... ☐

MONDAY

TUESDAY

WEDNESDAY

THURSDAY

FRIDAY

SATURDAY

SUNDAY

CHAPTER 7

BEDROOM

There's nothing like sinking into freshly laundered bed sheets at the end of a busy day. My bedroom is my sanctuary – I want it to be as relaxing an environment as possible, a place where I can feel at ease and get a good night's sleep. Fresh bedding promotes better sleep and wellbeing, as well as good hygiene by reducing dust mites and allergens. A clean and uncluttered bedroom also results in a calmer, more organised space, where you can both wind down in the evenings and find clothes quickly on busy mornings. Here are some tips on how to clean and create an orderly space in the bedroom.

QUICK CLEANING TIPS

- Make the bed every morning
- When leaving your room, remove items that don't live there
- Put away clothes – avoid teetering piles of clothes in one corner
- Keep your bedroom free of unnecessary clutter
- Make use of good storage, preferably out of sight
- Throw out any out-of-date make-up and beauty products

Beds

We spend a third of our lives in our beds so it's important to look after them to promote better sleep, good posture and a healthy body. As we sleep, sweat, body oils, bacteria and dust mites (which feed on dead skin cells) can quickly accumulate, so regular cleaning of bedding is essential.

Bedding and mattress

It's recommended to wash bedding – that's bed sheets, pillow-cases and duvet covers – once a week. You can get good results with a warm 40°C (100°F) wash and a good-quality detergent, although a hot 60°C (140°C) wash will kill germs and dust mites more effectively, especially on bedding used by infants or anyone with allergies or who is unwell. Always check the care labels of your bedding as some delicate fabrics like silk or certain synthetics may be damaged at high temperatures.

Instead of using fabric softener with your detergent, swap it for 60–120 ml (¼–½ cup) white vinegar, which softens fabric and is gentler on your bedding. You could also add a few drops of essential oil to the white vinegar, and there are some oils, like eucalyptus, which help to kill dust mites.

About once a month I give the mattress a quick vacuum to remove any dust, bacteria and other allergens. I have a mattress vacuum, but you could use a regular vacuum with an upholstery

attachment. It's also a good idea to use mattress and pillow protectors, which I'll wash every couple of months. These will protect the mattress and pillows from stains, dust mites and other allergens, so they'll last longer. (See page 242 for further details on removing stains.)

About every three months I'll sprinkle on to my mattress a generous layer of bicarbonate of soda, which is a great deodoriser, absorbing any moisture and resulting in a fresh smell. You could use a sieve or flour duster for this. I also add about 10 drops of essential oil – I love the smell of lavender and eucalyptus – leave it on for around thirty minutes, then vacuum it up, making sure I get into all the crevices and edges. (Ensure also that your vacuum has a HEPA [high-efficiency particulate air] filter.) You can leave the bicarbonate of soda to sit for up to eight hours, as the longer it sits the more odours and moisture it can absorb. Every few months you should rotate and, if you can, flip your mattress to prolong its life and ensure even wear.

Duvets and pillows

To keep duvets clean and fresh it's recommended you wash them every six months, or more frequently if you suffer from allergies or have pets. Check the care label, but most synthetic and some down or feather duvets can be machine-washed, although you may have to go to a launderette if your duvet is too big for your machine drum. After washing a duvet, make sure you dry it properly to prevent mould and mildew. If you're using a tumble dryer, add a dryer ball or hang the duvet outside on a sunny day, shaking and fluffing it periodically. In between washes, you can also air duvets and pillows outside in the sun, which will help to kill dust mites and keep them fresh.

Pillows should be washed every six months. In between

washes you can regularly fluff or reshape them to distribute their filling evenly. Most pillows, including scatter cushions, can be cleaned in the washing machine, but check the care label and follow the instructions for washing and drying. Here's how to wash pillows in the machine:

- It's best to wash two pillows at a time, as this helps to balance the load. To prevent ripping, put them in a pillowcase or pillow protector.
- Select a delicate or gentle cycle.
- Use a small amount of detergent and add vinegar to make your pillows fluffy and to neutralise any odours.
- Speed up the drying process by adding an extra spin (although check the care label first).
- Allow the pillows to dry fully to avoid any bacteria or mould growth.

If you're changing bed linen once a week, you want to get it done quickly. Here's a great hack for putting a duvet cover on in moments. There are a few online demonstrations of the method below, so check those out if you need a little help!

- Turn your duvet cover inside out and lay it on the bed, so that the opening is at the foot of the bed.
- Put the duvet on top, lining up the corners with the duvet cover.
- From the head of the bed, start rolling both all the way to the bottom of the bed.
- At the bottom, reach into the opening of the duvet cover at one end and flip it over the rolled-up duvet so it's right side out. Do the same on the other side.

- Then simply unroll the rest of the cover and duvet to the top of the bed. And that's it. So easy!

Headboard

Every month or so I'll refresh the fabric headboard on my bed with warm water and a few drops of dish soap. A good way to do this is to lightly dampen a cloth, wrap it around a saucepan lid and scrub the headboard. This way, you get a good purchase on the lid and it distributes the moisture evenly.

A good clean routine for your bed:

Daily – make bed
Weekly – change and wash bed linen
Monthly – clean headboard, vacuum mattress and mattress protector
Every three months – wash mattress protector and pillow protector, deodorise mattress
Every six months – wash duvet and pillows

Let's go over how you can give your main bedroom a thorough clean over a seven-day period.

Monday – dust hard surfaces and lampshades (try using a lint roller)
Tuesday – dust blinds/curtains and headboard
Wednesday – sort/clean make-up brushes and products
Thursday – vacuum, sweep or mop floors

179

Friday – sort through and declutter clothing

Saturday – clean windows (see pages 35 and 57 for the tools to make it easier)

Sunday – change bedding (see duvet cover hack, page 178) and vacuum/deodorize mattress

Make-up and beauty products

You might have a make-up or beauty routine, but do you have a cleaning routine for the products and tools you use? Similarly, you might cleanse your skin every day, but how often do you clean your make-up brush or beauty blender, where grease, bacteria and even mould can lurk. Here are some tips on how to clean items in your make-up bag or on your bedroom dressing table, all of which take just a few minutes.

Brushes

It's recommended to clean make-up brushes once a week and it's a quick five-minute job to do so. Put the bristles in warm water or micellar water to remove any excess product. Then place them on a make-up brush cleaning mat (which are widely available, or you could use any surface with ridges, like a soap tray), cover with baby shampoo or gentle soap, then rub and swirl the head of each brush, removing as much product as possible. Rinse under water until all the residue has gone. Squeeze out any moisture, reshape the bristles and lay on a towel to dry, preferably with the bristles hanging off the edge of a ledge to allow air circulation, or hang the brushes up to dry.

Sponges or beauty blenders

Make-up sponges need to be rinsed every day as bacteria and germs love damp, spongey places and you don't want to be spreading those germs on to your skin. Cut a well-used sponge in half and you might even see mould growing on the inside, which is pretty gross! Remember that make-up sponges are not meant to be washed and reused for months at a time, and should be replaced every one to three months.

Give your sponge/beauty blender a proper clean at least once a week by placing the sponge in a bowl or sink of warm water mixed with a few drops of liquid soap, and work into the sponge. Rinse and repeat. Then let it air-dry, preferably in a blender holder so it aerates properly; it will need a good few days to dry. This is another quick five-minute job.

Other make-up

Make-up products have expiration dates – see the table below for a guide to how long you should keep certain items. Go through your make-up bag every few months to see what needs throwing away and replacing.

HOW LONG TO KEEP PRODUCTS

Mascara – three to six months
Liquid eyeliner – six months
Eyeliner pencil – one year
Lipstick – two years
Lip liner – two years
Lip balm and gloss – one year
Cream blusher and eyeshadow – one year

Foundation – one to two years
Concealer – one to two years
Powder eyeshadow and blusher – two years

Here's how to clean and disinfect other make-up items, all of which take just minutes to do:

- Mascara – wipe the wand with a tissue every few uses. For a deeper clean, rinse under hot water and let the wand dry completely before reinserting it into the tube.
- Lipsticks – wipe with a clean tissue to remove the top layer. You could also dip the tip into rubbing alcohol or wipe with a disinfectant wipe.
- Eyeliners and lip liners – sharpen the pencil to remove the outside layer. Wipe the sharpener with a disinfectant wipe or rubbing alcohol.
- Powder products, like blushers, bronzers or eyeshadows – use a dry tissue to wipe away any loose powder, spritz with rubbing alcohol and allow to dry.
- Liquid products, like foundation – wipe off the top layer with a tissue or with a cotton swab dampened with rubbing alcohol.
- Wipe the exterior of all items, including palettes and compacts, with a disinfectant wipe or cloth dampened with rubbing alcohol.
- Make-up bags – remove all the items and shake out the loose debris or powder. Give the items a declutter, selecting which ones to clean, keep or chuck. If the bag is fabric, put it in the washing machine if it's machine-washable, or hand-wash in warm soapy water

and rinse. For non-fabric bags, wipe inside and out with a disinfectant wipe or cloth dampened with soapy water. Let it air-dry completely before using again.

. . . .

Top tips

Store make-up in a cool, dry place to prevent the build-up of bacteria. Always wash your hands before applying make-up so you don't transfer bacteria to your products and face.

. . . .

Hairbrushes

Remove stray hairs from hairbrushes every few days and do a deep-clean once a month, or more regularly if you use styling products. Hairbrushes also harbour bacteria, germs and dead skin cells, which will transfer to your hair, making it look greasy and lifeless.

To give a hairbrush a deep-clean, remove any hair, then put the brush in a sink or bowl of hot water with a scoop of bicarbonate of soda or a squirt of gentle shampoo. Leave it to soak for ten to fifteen minutes, during which time the bicarbonate of soda or shampoo will break down any oils or product build-up. (If your brush has a wooden handle, soak it just for a few minutes.) Scrub the bristles with an old toothbrush, getting into all the crevices, rinse in clean water, give it a good shake to remove excess water and leave to dry completely.

WELLBEING IN THE BEDROOM

Here are a few simple ways to enhance your bedroom so it feels like a calm space, promoting healthy sleep habits.

- Invest in a good-quality mattress, pillows and bedding for ultimate comfort and support.
- Keep the room cool: a temperature of 15–19°C (60–67°F) improves sleep quality.
- Avoid looking at phones or electronic devices an hour before going to bed. Instead read, write a journal, do some breathing exercises, or whatever relaxes you.
- Block out light, using blackout curtains or an eye mask.
- Reduce noise – invest in double-glazing, wear ear plugs, put on a white noise machine or listen to calming sounds.
- Keep decor relatively simple and use calming colours in the bedroom. Soft blues, greens, greys and neutrals are ideal.
- Keep clutter to a minimum and try to keep work or daytime activities separate to the bedroom.
- Sprinkle essential oils on to your mattress or headboard or make a DIY diffuser (see page 259).

Kids' bedrooms

When it comes to cleaning my son Oliver's bedroom, I usually give it a general tidy on a daily basis, putting away clothes, toys and books. As your child gets older, encourage them to make their beds, put away their toys and generally develop habits that will set them in good stead for later life. It's fine to have a bit of mess around them when they're playing, but if they make their bed or put away an item of clothing, tell them what a good job they've done and what a difference it makes to the room.

On a weekly basis, I change Oliver's bed sheets, vacuum the floor, dust hard surfaces and go through any clutter. Every month I pull out items of furniture and give a good vacuum or mop underneath, and dust the blinds.

Every few months I go through Oliver's toys, decluttering any he's grown out of. I also put some of his soft toys in the washing machine, plastic ones in the dishwasher, and some I'll disinfect, either wiping them with a disinfectant wipe or a cloth dipped in rubbing alcohol. Sometimes I'll use a sterilising fluid, filling a bucket or tray with warm water, adding a capful of liquid (such as Milton sterilising fluid) and soaking items like Lego for thirty minutes or so.

Make good use of storage in kids' rooms, with shelves, hanging pockets which the child can reach, as well as higher storage and boxes. In Oliver's room we currently have an ottoman bed, blanket box and shelves, but will no doubt add to this as he grows. Wall-mounted storage is always a good idea as it results in a less cluttered floor space.

BEDROOM CHECKLIST

DAILY

Make bed
Put away laundered clothes
Keep on top of clutter

WEEKLY

Change and wash bedding
Dust hard surfaces
Vacuum, sweep or mop floors

Clean mirrors or dust blinds/curtains

Wash make-up brushes or sponges

MONTHLY

Vacuum and turn mattress

Clean headboard

Sort through and clean make-up items

Wash hairbrush

Dust walls, corners and light fixtures

SEASONAL

Deodorise mattress

Wash duvets and pillows

Sort through and declutter clothing

Declutter and clean toys

NOTES

CHECKLIST

.... ☐

.... ☐

.... ☐

.... ☐

.... ☐

.... ☐

.... ☐

.... ☐

.... ☐

.... ☐

.... ☐

.... ☐

BEDROOM

.... ☐

.... ☐

.... ☐

.... ☐

.... ☐

.... ☐

.... ☐

.... ☐

.... ☐

.... ☐

.... ☐

.... ☐

.... ☐

.... ☐

.... ☐

.... ☐

MONDAY

TUESDAY

WEDNESDAY

THURSDAY

FRIDAY

SATURDAY

SUNDAY

CHAPTER 8

LIVING AREAS

The living room of our homes is often where we come to relax, lounge on a sofa and unwind from a busy day. At other times, it might be a hub of activity – during the day my living room is where my son Oliver plays, but come the evening it's more of a child-free zone. You might have a workspace in a corner or need plenty of space for a yoga session. Whatever the set-up, it's important your living room meets the needs of everyone in the household. This chapter provides tips on how to keep on top of the cleaning in your living room, as well as in other communal living areas, which are often busy spaces such as the entrance way, corridors and stairs.

QUICK CLEANING TIPS

- Plump up cushions, straighten covers and reset the room after use
- Take dirty crockery or items with you when you leave the room
- Make use of extendable dusters and dusting gloves
- A quick vacuum will make all the difference
- Good storage is a must, especially in the entrance way
- Have a few choice ornaments but don't keep adding to them
- Use a washable throw on the sofa if food and drink is consumed there

Living room

At the end of every day, I put away Oliver's toys so I can return the room from playroom to living room; to a place that feels a little more ordered and relaxing for the evening wind-down. Before I head to bed, I straighten sofa cushions and pillows, put the remote by the TV, removing any glasses or items as I go. It's a quick reset of the living area, which takes no time at all and makes it a pleasant space to return to the next day.

I give the living room a vacuum at least once a week. I dust and clean hard surfaces once a week, give the sofa a deep-clean once a month, along with cleaning walls and skirting boards. Here's a bit more detail on the various tasks, which you can break down into manageable chunks of cleaning.

Floors

If you have hard floors, give them a vacuum or sweep regularly and mop once a week using hot water and a little dish soap. For wooden floors, I recommend using a spin mop or flat-headed mop with dual reservoir, making sure the mop head is damp rather than wet. Once a month or every few weeks, pull out the furniture and clean the floors thoroughly.

If you have carpets, regular vacuuming will keep them in good condition, improve the look of the room and cut down on allergens. Make sure you have a vacuum with good suction, preferably with a HEPA (high-efficency particulate air) filter, which can capture pollen, dust, dirt and some viruses and bacteria, and multiple attachments. I have a cordless vacuum and it's been a real game-changer for me – I used to hate vacuuming, but I enjoy it now and find it so much easier to move around the house without having to worry about a lead.

To add fragrance before you vacuum, you could sprinkle cinnamon powder over your carpet, or alternatively 130 g (½ cup) bicarbonate of soda mixed with 20–30 drops of essential oils of your choice.

....

Top tip

To remove indentations from heavy furniture on carpets or rugs, place an ice cube on the spot, allow it to melt and tease up the pile with a brush or cocktail stick.

....

Steam cleaning is a really effective way to clean carpets. You could use your own device – I use an upright steam mop and carpet attachment – hire a steam cleaning machine or get a professional in to do the job. (The latter is recommended if you've just moved into a home or you have large areas that need deep-cleaning – a professional service can literally make your carpets look as good as new.) See page 242 for more information on spot cleaning carpet stains.

When it comes to rugs, I vacuum mine at least once a week. To remove any odours, once a month I sprinkle on bicarbonate of soda and a few drops of essential oil and leave it for around fifteen minutes before vacuuming it up. You can also go down the traditional route of hanging up your rugs in the garden and beating them with a broom or big stick – it's amazing how much dust and other debris can come out even after you've vacuumed them!

MINI CLEAN ROUTINE FOR FLOORS

Daily – sweep or vacuum high-traffic areas

Weekly – vacuum carpets and rugs thoroughly and sweep/
mop hard floors

Monthly – deodorise carpets or rugs, pull out furniture and
vacuum

Seasonal – steam clean or wash/spot clean carpets

Hard surfaces

Once a week I give the hard surfaces in my living room – tables, mantlepiece, shelves and ledges – a good dust. I like to use my damp duster as it really picks up the dust, spraying first with my DIY dusting spray (see page 36). You can also use a microfibre cloth or dusting glove.

I also run a lint roller over my lampshades and, once a month, or as needed, I give my plants a dust. You could use a make-up brush on the leaves, or dusting gloves would also work well here.

For the television and any electrical equipment and wires – all of which seem to attract dust like nothing else – I use my static extendable duster, but again you could use dusting gloves or a microfibre cloth. To clean the screen, use a clean microfibre cloth to wipe away smudges and fingerprints – don't spray liquid or solution on to a TV screen. You can use a dampened cloth for any other boxes, stands or panels underneath.

Walls

Every month or so I give the walls and
fixtures a dust and clean. Using an extendable static duster, I dust the corners of
the ceiling and coving and then move
down to light fixtures, door frames, picture
rails and tops of mirrors, before running the
duster along the skirting boards. (Remember, always
work from top to bottom, as dust, cobwebs and dirt will
fall as you dust.) I then dust the ceilings and walls with my
Flash Speed Mop fitted with a static dust pad.

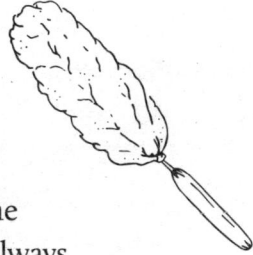

Top tip

To dust a ceiling fan, first switch it off, then grab an old pillowcase and slide it over one of the blades. When you pull it back,
any dust or debris will fall inside the case rather than on the
furniture or floor below. Repeat with the other blades, then
shake the pillowcase outside.

As our walls often get covered in mucky fingerprints (all about
toddler level!), I give them a wash every month or so. I use a flat-
headed mop and warm water with just a few drops of dish soap
so it's gentle enough not to affect the paintwork and I can put as
much or as little pressure on the wall as I like. I also run the mop
along the skirting boards, where dirt can accumulate.

To dust and wipe down light fixtures, make sure they are
switched off, then use a microfibre cloth that has been dampened
in soapy water. You could also use dusting gloves for this job.

Let's go over how you can give your living areas a
thorough clean over a seven-day period.

Monday – vacuum floors and dust/mop skirting boards
Tuesday – clean windows
Wednesday – dust and mop walls, dust ceiling lights/fans
Thursday – deep-clean sofas and chairs
Friday – dust surfaces and workspaces, clean and disinfect
  phones/computers
Saturday – clean stairs, entrance ways and spot clean
  carpet stains
Sunday – dust blinds or vacuum/steam curtains

Sofa

Sofas and armchairs see a lot of action. Cushions can become misshapen, crumbs and debris can accumulate, and, as the focal point of a room, they can really impact the overall look. On a daily basis, I reshape and plump up the cushions and reassemble any throws or blankets so the sofa looks generally in good shape next time I return to the room.

I give the sofa a good vacuum on a weekly or monthly basis, taking off all the cushions and vacuuming up any debris – it's amazing what you can find under the cushions (bits of cereal in my case)! Vacuum along the seams and right down between the cushions.

Giant lint rollers are great for picking up any pet hairs on sofas and chairs. I use a lint scraper on the stairs, but you could also use one on your upholstery if you have pet hair and fluff you need to remove.

To give a fabric sofa a deep-clean – a job that will take more than five minutes – bicarbonate of soda is usually safe to use, but you might want to test it out on a hidden area first. Put around 500 ml (generous 2 cups) warm water in a bowl, add 1 tablespoon of bicarbonate of soda and 1 tablespoon of dish soap. Wet and wring out a microfibre cloth and wipe the fabric, although I find it also works well to tie the cloth around a saucepan lid before scrubbing. That way you distribute the moisture as you glide it across the fabric – scrubbing by hand can sometimes result in wetting the fabric a little too much. Rinse the cloth when it starts to look discoloured.

If you have washable covers, remove and wash them once or twice a year or whenever needed.

Steam cleaners work brilliantly on sofas as they don't require harsh chemicals which could discolour the fabric, and the steam kills bacteria, germs and allergens. It's best to use your steam cleaner regularly, lifting any stains as quickly as possible. Follow the user manual to set the right temperature and amount of water for your sofa. Usually, the steam will loosen any dirt or gunk, but you might need to use a brush or scrubber to dislodge any stubborn residues.

I also have a Bissell Spot Cleaner machine, which quickly and easily lifts away stains or accidental spills on upholstery. They are not cheap but they are really effective and you can also use them on rugs, the stairs and in the car. If you have young children and pets and like a spotless house, then you might consider it a good investment.

If you have a leather sofa, vacuum it and then wipe it down with a damp, but not sopping, cloth that has been dipped in a solution of warm water and a mild soap like Castile or saddle soap. Water can discolour or stain leather, so make sure you follow the care instructions and use a specialist cleaner if in doubt.

MINI CLEAN ROUTINE FOR SOFAS

Daily – reshape cushions, plump up pillows and reassemble throws or blankets

Weekly – vacuum and run a lint roller over it

Monthly or seasonal – wash or steam clean sofa, spot clean stains

Twice a year – wash covers and pillowcases

Curtains, blinds and shutters

I have curtains on my living room windows, both sheer and thick thermal curtains. Once a month I'll give them a shake where they hang to remove dust and run a lint roller over them. Taking them down and shaking outside will also remove a lot of dust that has accumulated. I like also to give them a steam clean, which I can do without having to take them down, and most steam cleaners come with a detachable head for fabrics. Alternatively, aim to wash your curtains at least once a year: you can put them in the washing machine if they are machine washable, or take them to the dry cleaners – check the care label. Most net curtains can be machine-washed and you should aim to wash them at least twice a year.

If you have shutters on your windows, close them and wipe them down with a microfibre cloth or damp duster on both sides, and always work from the top to the bottom. You could also use a dusting glove to wipe each slat, top and bottom, shaking off dust as you go. To wipe off marks, use warm soapy water and avoid chemical cleaning products on natural wood shutters as they could damage the colour of the wood and lead to warping. Wipe away any excess moisture with a microfibre cloth.

For Venetian blinds, dust each slat from top to bottom, using a microfibre cloth or dusting glove, wiping the top and underside of the slats. Wipe off any marks with a cloth dipped in warm soapy water. You can also vacuum blinds using a suitable attachment or nozzle, on a low suction setting.

For fabric blinds, you can usually vacuum them with an upholstery attachment or dust them with an extendable static duster. You could also steam clean them or wipe them down with a damp cloth, or you may need to take them to the dry cleaners, depending on the fabric and care label instruction.

Note that most of the above cleaning tasks will take longer than five minutes, so tackle these jobs only when you know you have the time.

Workspace

Work areas and desks can attract mess and clutter, which can dominate a living space if you don't keep on top of it. Keep clutter to a minimum, give the desk a quick tidy at the end of a work session and invest in good storage.

Dust your workspace at least once a week. Run a damp duster or microfibre cloth over the desk and an extendable static duster along the cables and socket area, or use a vacuum to remove any dust or fluff. You should also do the same with the chair.

To clean computer equipment, shut down the power and unplug anything electrical. Give the keyboard (if it's separate to your computer) a good clean at least once a month. Turn it upside down and gently shake out any crumbs. (Better yet, avoid eating over your keyboard or invest in a keyboard cover – food and liquid should be kept well away from keyboards!) Then very lightly moisten a microfibre cloth with plain water or rubbing alcohol and gently wipe the surface. You could also use a cotton swab dipped in rubbing alcohol to gently clean between the keys, or use a make-up brush. Allow to air-dry and use the same method to gently wipe your computer mouse.

To clean the monitor, switch off the power source and gently wipe the screen using a soft, lint-free microfibre cloth – avoid abrasive cloths or paper towels. If there are any smudges, you could add a little rubbing alcohol to your cloth and gently sweep the screen. The glass on some computers (namely Apple products) should be cleaned with the polishing cloth that came with the device, so always check the manufacturer's care instructions.

Mobile phones (and remote controls) should also be disinfected at least once a week – they are in our hands all the time so get covered in skin oils, bacteria and germs. Turn off your phone before cleaning it, and Apple recommends wiping the outside with a 70 per cent isopropyl alcohol wipe or soft, lint-free cloth, keeping all liquids, cleaning products, compressed air and sprays well away as they could damage the phone. You should avoid getting moisture in any of the openings.

QUICK FIVE-MINUTE CLEANS

There are items around the home which often get forgotten about but are probably covered in germs. Once a week spend five minutes disinfecting items such as light switches, door handles and remote controls. Wipe them with a microfibre cloth, dampened with rubbing alcohol or DIY disinfectant spray.

Fact check

What is rubbing alcohol?

Rubbing alcohol or surgical spirit is a diluted form of isopropyl alcohol. The concentration of many brands of rubbing alcohol is 70 per cent, whereas isopropyl alcohol is 100 per cent. Both are disinfectants and have antibacterial properties but because isopropyl alcohol is undiluted it is a more hazardous product and should not be kept in the home.

Radiators

To clean radiators, I tend to blast out the dust with a hair dryer and then vacuum it up. You can also use a radiator brush specially made for this job. I wash radiators with a steam cleaner, or you can wipe them down with a cloth and soapy water.

Top tip

When washing your radiators, adding a few drops of essential oil to your soapy water will fill your living area with a lovely fragrance!

Entrance way and stairs

This is of course the first area you or any guests come into on entering your home, so it's important to keep it clean, uncluttered and welcoming. Keep the entrance way well lit, invest in plenty of hooks, cupboards and storage (see page 116), and for hygiene it's always best to remove your shoes before entering the house.

Vacuum the entrance way and corridors regularly, including any mats or rugs.

The walls in these areas can get particularly grubby so give them a regular dust and mop, using the same methods as in the living room. You could always paint these areas in washable paint for extra ease.

Keep the stairs free of clutter and give them a regular vacuum as they take a lot of traffic. Use a crevice nozzle to get into the risers and corners, and I like to use a lint scraper to remove any hair and fluff. Dust the banisters with an extendable static duster and wipe them down with a DIY disinfectant or dusting spray (see pages 42 and 36), depending on whether you have exposed wood.

Above all, be careful when vacuuming the stairs, which you should do from the bottom to the top to prevent the vacuum (and you) toppling down the stairs. If you have any mobility issues, it's best to ask for help here or invest in a lighter hand-held (and preferably cordless) vacuum for the stairs.

LIVING AREA CHECKLIST

DAILY

Clear up clutter, clear away crockery and put away toys
Straighten sofa and cushions

WEEKLY

Vacuum living room, entrance way and stairs
Dust hard surfaces
Vacuum sofa and chairs

Clean and disinfect phones and computer equipment

Dust office space

MONTHLY

Deep-clean sofa and armchairs

Dust and mop walls

Pull out all furniture and mop/vacuum the floor

Dust and mop ceiling, coves and skirting boards

Deodorise rugs and carpets

Dust and clean light fixtures

Dust, wipe down or vacuum shutters or blinds

SEASONAL

Steam clean carpets

Remove and wash sofa covers or steam clean

Steam or dry clean curtains or blinds

Clean windows

Dust and wipe radiators

NOTES

....

....

....

....

....

....

....

....

....

....

....

CHECKLIST

.... ☐

.... ☐

.... ☐

.... ☐

.... ☐

.... ☐

.... ☐

.... ☐

.... ☐

.... ☐

.... ☐

.... ☐

MONDAY

TUESDAY

WEDNESDAY

THURSDAY

FRIDAY

SATURDAY

SUNDAY

CHAPTER 9

LAUNDRY AND IRONING

Keeping on top of laundry is a key part of any household routine. It's an area that can quickly mount up if not dealt with regularly – and nobody likes great piles of dirty laundry or ironing, especially when you can't find what you need on a busy morning. By following the tips below, the laundry can, however, become part of your daily routine without taking over your life, making you feel more organised and in control. After all, you deserve those clean sheets or fresh-smelling shirts, so go wash!

Speed up your washing routine

Do a laundry-related task most days – wash a load of clothes or fold some dry clothes and put them away. Many washing machines have a half load or quick wash setting, so you can do smaller, daily washes as part of your everyday routine. Try turning down the temperature of your wash – many detergents work just as well at a cooler 30°C (85°F) wash – which will reduce the energy consumption. Remember also that laundry labels give the maximum temperature for washing, not the recommended temperature.

Don't assume all your clothing needs to be washed after every wear. Many items in your wardrobe can be worn more than once, and in fact overlaundering some fabrics, like wool or denim, can reduce their lifespan (see pages 216–217 for how often you should wash certain items). You could create an area or hanging space in your bedroom or wardrobe for garments already worn but which could be worn again before washing. Avoid throwing them on a chair – or the floor – in a messy pile. Instead, hang them on a hook or a rail and go through them once a week.

Instead of washing, you can freshen up clothing by removing them from your wardrobe, hanging them outside in the fresh air and steaming with a hand-held garment steamer. This can remove odours and most bacteria, and smooth out creases – which is perfect if you're travelling or away from home. You can also brush them with a lint roller or clothes brush and even sponge off any visible marks.

Buy clothes that are easy to wash and to care for. To avoid hand-washing, which can be time-consuming, or paying for dry cleaning, buy clothes that you can wash in your machine on a regular cycle.

Separate your laundry into dark and light or white items. You could also separate by fabric (cotton, synthetic, wool or delicate) or run a separate, hotter 60°C (140°F) wash for towels or bed sheets.

To avoid tissue explosions, make sure all pockets are emptied. Ensure fastenings are zipped or buttoned up to stop them clanking about in the machine, and to avoid fading turn dark coloured items inside out.

Use the detergent that works best in your machine and on your clothing – I prefer liquid detergent and use white vinegar instead of fabric softener. I put between 60–120 ml (¼ –½ cup) vinegar in the conditioner dispenser drawer of my machine and it softens and freshens my clothes and is great with both white and coloured fabrics.

Don't overload your washing machine as your clothes will come out less clean, more wrinkled and it puts stress on your machine.

To avoid clothes getting tangled up together as they wash, put socks, underwear and other small items in separate mesh bags (see page 218).

Check the laundry label – it is there for a reason! How often have you inadvertently shrunk a jumper or deflated a puffer coat because you failed to read the label? The guide overleaf lists all the laundry labels and what they mean. Some smartphones and laundry apps will provide information on certain symbols if you take a photo of them.

Pre-treating

Before putting things directly into the wash, I often pre-treat garments if they're looking discoloured or stained. (While pre-treating involves soaking and letting products work, actual hands-on work is minimal.) White vinegar is a really effective stain remover – just spray it directly on to a stain or mark, making sure the vinegar has really seeped in, let it sit for at least fifteen minutes, then run a normal wash cycle.

Some stains benefit from being soaked in cold water first and it's always best to deal with stains as quickly as possible, blotting the affected area quickly with a paper towel or cloth to soak up any remaining grease or liquid. (See chapter ten for further information on stain removal.)

For greasy food stains, again it's best to get to them quickly, grab a tissue and soak up any excess grease, then dab on some dish soap or any kind of detergent, let it sit for five to ten minutes, give it a scrub and then put it in the wash. For really stubborn stains I might also

LAUNDRY GUIDE

Washing symbol	Wash at or below 30°C (USA, •)	Wash at or below 40°C (USA, ••)	Wash at or below 50°C (USA, •••)	Wash at or below 60°C (USA, ••••)	Hand wash
Do not wash	Bleaching symbol	Bleaching with chlorine allowed	Non-chlorine bleach when needed	Do not bleach	Do not bleach
Tumble drying symbol	Tumble drying (low temperature)	Tumble drying (normal)	Do not tumble dry	Drying symbol	Line dry
Dry flat	Drip dry	Dry in the shade	Line dry in the shade	Dry flat in shade	Drip dry in shade
Ironing symbol	Iron at low temperature	Iron at medium temperature	Iron at high temperature	Do not iron	Professional cleaning symbol
Dry clean, hydrocarbon solvent only (HCS)	Gentle cleaning with hydrocarbon solvents	Very gentle cleaning with hydrocarbon solvents	Dry clean, tetrachloroethylene (PCE) only	Gentle cleaning with PCE	Very gentle cleaning with PCE
Do not dry clean	Professional wet cleaning	Gentle wet cleaning	Very gentle wet cleaning	Do not wet clean	

rub a Vanish stain remover soap bar straight on to the mark prior to washing, so the soap's enzymes get to work to remove the stain.

Alternatively, you can mix two parts bicarbonate of soda with one part water to create a paste, then spread over the stain. Let it dry, then wipe it off and put in the wash as normal. You can also add bicarbonate of soda to your detergent, which will help to brighten and whiten fabrics.

For whites that are looking grey or discoloured, I might soak them in oxi powder – I use the Vanish Oxi Action products – for at least thirty minutes before putting them in the washing machine with my usual detergent. You could also add 270 g (1 cup) bicarbonate of soda into the drum or 60–120 ml (¼–½ cup) white vinegar where you would usually put fabric softener. Hanging your whites outside in the sun can also help to naturally bleach them to keep them bright.

To stop dark colours fading, add 270 g (1 cup) table salt to the drum before washing with your usual detergent, and 60–120 ml (¼–½ cup) white vinegar instead of fabric softener to keep the colour locked in for longer.

Collars and cuffs can be problem areas, where sweat, make-up or natural oils from skin can accumulate. Rub some shampoo or dish soap into these areas and let sit for thirty minutes before washing as normal.

For sweat stains, spray on white vinegar, letting it really seep into the stain, or cover with a paste of bicarbonate of soda and water and let it sit for at least twenty minutes before washing.

To soften towels, fill a large sink or container with hot water and add soda crystals – about 120 g (½ cup) soda crystals per 4.5 litres (1 gallon) water. Let the soda crystals dissolve, submerge the towels and allow to soak for several hours or overnight. The soda crystals will strip the fibres of the built-up residue that causes them to feel rough. Rinse the towels thoroughly in clean water and then wash them in the washing machine with your usual detergent, swapping out fabric softener with white vinegar.

HOW OFTEN SHOULD YOU WASH CLOTHES?

After each wear

Underwear

Tights and socks

T-shirts

Shirts

Gym clothes

Every three wears

Pyjamas

Bras

Trousers

Sweaters

Dresses

Every five to ten wears

Jeans

Skirts

As and when

Chunky jumpers

Dressing gowns

Coats

Hats

Gloves and scarves

HOW OFTEN SHOULD YOU WASH HOUSEHOLD ITEMS?

Every day

    Tea towels

    Face cloths

Every week

    Microfibre cloths

    Towels

    Bed sheets

    Duvet covers

    Pillowcases

Every month

    Bathmats

    Mop heads

Every three to six months

    Cushion covers

    Mattress protector

    Shower curtain

    Throws

    Net curtains

Seasonally

    Pillows

    Cushions

    Blankets

    Duvet

Top tips

- Wash your jeans every five to ten wears. Use a gentle 30°C (85°F) cycle to avoid shrinking and fading.
- If you have machine-washable net curtains, put them on a cool cycle with a tablespoon of white vinegar and detergent and then hang up to dry.
- Make use of laundry mesh bags, which are designed to hold delicate or small items during a washing machine cycle. They can prevent items such as silk, lace or lingerie from snagging, tearing or stretching during the wash. They are also a really useful way of keeping small items such as socks, bras or baby clothes together, which can get lost or tangled up with larger loads. You can also buy special bags for pet items such as bedding and towels to stop pet hairs clogging up the machine.
- If you get chewing gum stuck on fabric, freezing it makes it less sticky and easier to remove. Once frozen, use a blunt knife or spoon to gently scrape it off.
- There are all sorts of clever accessories you can buy to facilitate doing the laundry, including an ingenious cap washer frame, which will protect the shape of your baseball cap in the machine. You can also buy a bed sheet detangler, a rubber device that attaches to your sheets and stops them tangling, twisting and balling up, reducing wrinkles and creases.

Trainers

Here are some tips on cleaning trainers. Many types of trainers, including those made of cotton, canvas, nylon or polyester, can be put in a washing machine, although check the care label or any online advice from the manufacturer before doing so. Suede or leather trainers, or those with beading or rope soles, should be cleaned by hand.

If you are washing them in your washing machine, it's best to put them in a padded mesh bag or inside a pillowcase along with towels to stop them banging around the drum.

Here's a guide to how to clean trainers in a washing machine:

1. Bang the trainers together and brush off any dried mud or dirt. Remove the laces and insoles and gently scrub any stained areas with dish soap and water.

2. Place in a mesh bag and put the laces and insoles either in a smaller mesh bag or wash separately in soapy water and vinegar (clean laces will instantly transform the look of your trainers). Add a few towels to the washing machine drum.

3. Wash on a gentle or delicate cycle at a maximum of 30°C (85°F) to avoid shrinkage or distortion. Avoid a spin cycle.

4. Remove the trainers from the mesh bag and reshape them. To help with this, you could stuff them with paper towels or cloths, which will also help to absorb any moisture.

5. Let them dry naturally – do not tumble dry them, put them out in hot sun or dry with a hair dryer, all of which can misshape them. Put your laces and insoles in and enjoy your clean, fresh-smelling trainers.

Top tip

If you want to whiten and brighten your trainers by hand, scrub them all over with an old toothbrush and toothpaste. Leave the toothpaste on for ten minutes, then wipe away.

Other surprising items you can put in the washing machine to save time: soft toys, backpacks, material lunch bags, oven gloves, reusable shopping bags, plastic toys (in a mesh bag), machine washable curtains, mop heads, head bands.

Washing machine

Thank goodness for washing machines – but remember they need cleaning too. Over time, detergent residue, as well as odours, bacteria and mould, can build, which can affect the performance of your washing machine and transfer to your clothes. To prevent any problems, it's best to give your machine a good clean every three to six months or whenever you notice any build-up of odours or mildew.

Once a month, it's recommended to run the machine empty on a hot wash – or run a self-cleaning cycle if you have one – and give the detergent drawer a quick clean with soapy water. Between washes, it's also a good idea to leave the door and detergent drawer open to prevent odours.

To deep-clean your washing machine, follow these steps. This job will take ten to fifteen minutes plus a wash cycle. Remember to turn off and unplug the washing machine for safety when you're cleaning it by hand.

1. Remove the detergent and conditioner drawer and give it a good clean in soapy water. A toothbrush or sonic scrubber might be useful here. Leave to dry, then replace.

2. Most washing machines have a filter which catches all the loose bits during a wash. To clean or unblock it, locate the filter, which is often located on a front panel (refer to the washing machine's manual). Place a bowl or bucket under the filter to catch any water and then open the panel door and unscrew or remove the filter. Remove any bits in the filter using an old toothbrush, then rinse the filter in equal parts soapy water and vinegar. Dry and replace the filter.

3. Wipe down the door seal with equal parts water and vinegar.

4. Wipe down the door and the front of the washing machine.

5. Add 500 g (2½ cups) soda crystals to the drum and 240 ml (1 cup) white vinegar to the drawer (I always pop in cleaning cloths too to give them a freshen up).

6. Run a hot cycle and you're done!

. . . .

Top tip

You can also clean and deodorise your washing machine drum with lemon and toothpaste. Cut a lemon in half, add a swirl of toothpaste on each

half, throw into the drum and pop on a quick hot wash. The toothpaste removes dirt and grime and the antibacterial properties of the lemon will cut down limescale build-up.

....

Tumble dryer

If you have a tumble dryer at home, there are various quick and easy ways to look after it and keep it working efficiently and safely.

Don't be tempted to overload your tumble dryer. Doing so puts stress on the machine, reduces airflow, prolongs drying times and adds to the energy consumption.

Use appropriate settings and remove items promptly to prevent wrinkles and minimise the need for ironing.

After every use, remove lint and fluff from the lint filter or trap – which is usually located inside the door rim or behind a panel on the front of the dryer – using a soft brush or vacuum attachment. (Whichever tool you use, keep it nearby because you'll be using it often.)

Occasionally wipe down the drum with a damp cloth to remove residue or lint build-up, and to banish any odours.

Fabric softeners

Tumble dryer balls make a good, eco-friendly alternative to artificial fabric softeners or tumble dryer sheets. The best ones are made of wool and naturally soak up excess water and bounce around the dryer softening clothes. By improving the air flow in the drum, dryer balls shorten dry times and lower your energy bill, and they can also

prevent bed sheets tangling. Use three balls for small to medium loads, five balls for large loads.

For fragrance, you could add essential oils, such as lavender, lemon and eucalyptus, adding 2–3 drops per ball.

. . . .

Top tips

- Always check the care labels on your clothing as different fabrics require different temperatures and drying times.
- Choose the lowest temperature setting for delicate fabrics and remove items promptly when dry as overdrying can shrink clothes or cause damage.
- Shake out clothes before putting them in the dryer. This helps them to dry more evenly and removes any wrinkles.
- Put a dry hand towel in with your damp items. The dry cloth will absorb the moisture and speed up drying times.

. . . .

Deep-cleaning

To keep your tumble dryer in good working order, it's advisable to deep-clean it every three to six months. Here's how (although every appliance is different, so check your manual). This task will take longer than five minutes so tackle only on less busy days!

1. For safety, switch off and unplug the power source to the tumbler dryer. Wash the lint filter under the tap and use a vacuum on a low setting to clean out the lint filter housing. Make sure the filter is completely dry before putting it back in.

2. Before you reinsert the filter, clean the filter drawer or condenser. Wipe clean the surfaces of the filter housing by hand or with a vacuum cleaner set on low. If the foam pad looks dirty, rinse it under a tap and dry.
3. Give the drum a wipe down with a soft cloth using equal parts vinegar and water.
4. Wipe down the front, sides and back of the machine.
5. Clean the exhaust vent and hose. Use a vent brush or vacuum cleaner attachment to reach into the vent and remove any blockages. You might need a screwdriver to remove any screws securing the vent or hose. It is recommended to clean the vent or hose every six to twelve months, or if you notice clogging – doing so improves the efficiency of the dryer and reduces the risk of fire. If you don't feel confident doing this, you can always get in professional help.

Ironing

Unless you love to iron – and believe it or not there are people out there who do – for many of us ironing is that one extra chore we could do without. But there are lots of ways to speed up the process, or cut down or even banish that ironing pile! These include:

- Buy clothes in a fabric that requires minimal or no ironing.
- Fold or hang up garments as soon as they have dried. For heavier items, like jumpers or long dresses, let gravity pull out those wrinkles.
- Steaming is a quick and easy way to remove creases and wrinkles. A garment steamer can remove wrinkles from most fabrics, including delicates like silk, wool

and synthetics, although it's sometimes best to test a small area first. You can also steam items while they're hanging, making them perfect for curtains.

- Make use of your tumble dryer – a cooler setting will prevent creases setting. You can also spray DIY crease release spray (see below) on to dry clothes and toss in the dryer for five minutes.
- Invest in a good-quality iron with a steam function and variable settings as well as a sturdy, padded ironing board.
- Iron garments when slightly damp. Moisture helps to relax the fibres and makes ironing easier and quicker. For stubborn creases make up a DIY crease release spray using equal parts white vinegar and water and 15 drops of your favourite essential oil.
- Iron clothes inside out to avoid sheen on dark clothes.
- Check care labels and start with low-temperature items first, like silk, and move on to items that need higher heat. For really fragile items, cover with a clean tea towel and iron.

Top tip

If you spot a stain, don't iron over it as the heat will embed the stain even more. Soak the garment in cold water with a drop of white vinegar and wash again.

To keep your iron in good working condition:

- Empty out the water reservoir after use so limescale doesn't build up. Make sure the iron is completely cool when you put it away.

- Regularly clean the underside/soleplate of your iron to remove mineral deposits and gunk. Wipe with a damp cloth and mild detergent. For tougher residues, use an old toothbrush and put toothpaste on the underside. Leave for ten minutes and wipe off.
- Check the steam vents and clear out any blockages with a cocktail stick or similar.

LAUNDRY CHECKLIST

DAILY

Do a laundry-related task: put a wash on, or fold or put away dried clothes

If using a tumble dryer, remove lint and fluff from filter or traps

WEEKLY

Empty the water reservoir of your iron

Wash out the lint filter of your tumble dryer

MONTHLY

Give the washing machine detergent drawers a clean and run a self-cleaning cycle or hot wash

Wipe tumble dryer drum

Check and clean the soleplate of your iron

SEASONAL

Deep-clean your washing machine

Deep-clean your tumble dryer

NOTES

....

....

....

....

....

....

....

....

....

....

....

CHECKLIST

- .... ☐
- .... ☐
- .... ☐
- .... ☐
- .... ☐
- .... ☐
- .... ☐
- .... ☐
- .... ☐
- .... ☐
- .... ☐
- .... ☐

LAUNDRY AND IRONING

.... ☐

.... ☐

.... ☐

.... ☐

.... ☐

.... ☐

.... ☐

.... ☐

.... ☐

.... ☐

.... ☐

.... ☐

.... ☐

.... ☐

.... ☐

MONDAY

TUESDAY

WEDNESDAY

THURSDAY

FRIDAY

SATURDAY

SUNDAY

CHAPTER 10

PESTS, PETS AND STUBBORN STAINS

n this chapter we get down and dirty. We're talking about the grubby, sometimes forgotten areas of our homes, as well as those uninvited guests – insects, rodents and pests of all kinds – that occasionally make an unwelcome appearance. In addition, our pets, much as we love them, can add to that cleaning to-do list, and stains and spills are often unavoidable. Thankfully, there are lots of quick and effective ways to prevent and deal with these problem areas.

QUICK CLEANING TIPS

- Clean up spills immediately
- Sweep up or vacuum crumbs or food
- Avoid leaving food out uncovered
- Remove dirty crockery from rooms
- Keep surfaces clean
- Deal with stains quickly

Pests

Let's start with a topic I'm often asked about: pests! No one likes a house full of flies or – and I can barely write it – rodents, and there are certain times of the year when every corner of the house seems to have a spider making itself at home. So how can you deal with and deter these mini-beasts quickly and definitively? Here are some quick and easy methods.

Insects

Flies are probably the most common intruders in our homes, especially in hot weather when we have doors and windows open. There are also ants (the walking and flying kind), wasps, which can really be a nuisance, and various types of beetles that can find their way into cupboards and drawers. Once these insects get into your home, it's often difficult to get rid of them, so prevention is key. Good cleaning habits already outlined in this book will help prevent insect infestations. Here are some extra tips:

- Don't leave food out, particularly overripe fruit or rotting food which can attract flies.
- Clean up sticky spills and crumbs quickly from surfaces, floors and tabletops.
- Don't leave dirty crockery around – ants and flies in particular love sweet, sugary spills and fizzy drink cans.
- Wipe down kitchen surfaces with a clean cloth, spraying with a DIY all-purpose cleaner (see page 35) or a solution made up of equal parts water and white vinegar, which is a good insect deterrent (though avoid vinegar on granite or some other stone surfaces).
- Sweep, mop and vacuum floors regularly.
- If defrosting food, make sure it's sealed and covered up.

- Wash out pet bowls after use and clean around them.
- Empty bins regularly and keep them clean, making sure the lids are down, to prevent flies and other critters getting in and laying eggs.
- Make up a natural deterrent spray of 240 ml (1 cup) water and 5–10 drops of peppermint, tea tree or rosemary essential oil, the scent of which insects dislike. Spray it on window ledges, in corners or wherever insects seem to be getting in. (Always research your oils, however, and be careful with them around pets.)
- When mopping floors, add orange essential oil to your soapy water. The smell of orange deters insects and it's a less overpowering smell than peppermint and tea tree so it's perfect for larger surfaces like floors. Check the recommended dosage for how much to use – if nothing else, your house will smell amazing!

Spiders

I'm always keen to keep spider numbers down in my home and I've received all sorts of tips from followers on ways to get rid of them! The natural deterrent spray given above will work equally well with spiders, but I've also learnt that spiders hate the smell of cinnamon, so I occasionally place the odd cinnamon stick close to where I've spotted them. Regular cleaning and the removal of webs and food sources will also cut down your spider population, as will keeping on top of clutter as spiders love to hide in messy areas.

Tradition has it that spiders also hate conkers, so you could try scattering a few on window ledges or in corners – some people swear by them but, like cinnamon sticks, I don't think there's scientific proof they work. (Conkers are toxic to some animals so take care with anything you put around the home, especially if you have pets or young children.)

Moths

Clothes moths are a particular nuisance, principally because they ruin jumpers and garments made of natural fibres such as wool, silk and cashmere. Moths love undisturbed, dark areas like wardrobes, drawers and attics, where they lay eggs, and it's not the moths but their larvae that munch through your favourite silk cardigans.

. . . .

HOW TO PREVENT MOTHS

- Wash clothes regularly, especially those made of natural fibres. Hot temperatures can kill moths and their larvae, as can steam cleaning, although dry cleaning is the most effective way of killing the larvae. Freezing garments, followed by a usual washing cycle, is another good way to kill moth larvae – place the garment in an airtight bag, freeze for three days to a week, and then wash as normal.
- Occasionally deep-clean closets and drawers, removing all items. Spray with a mixture of essential oils – lavender, cedarwood or eucalyptus is recommended – or place scent bags made up of dried rosemary, cloves, thyme or bay leaves to deter moths.

- Store off-season or infrequently worn clothes, especially any woollen or silk items, in airtight containers or vacuum-sealed bags. You could also pack some cinnamon sticks in with them.

. . . .

Rodents

As with insects, the best way to prevent mice or rats coming into the house is to avoid leaving any scraps of food or dirty crockery out, cleaning up pet bowls regularly and dealing with any food or drink spills straightaway. Keeping a clean house is the best way to prevent rodents, but if you do suffer from an infestation – and remember, mice and their progeny can produce 200 offspring a year! – get professional help. Or you can always get a cat!

. . . .

Top tip

Rodents have a very good sense of smell, so strong scents like peppermint oil are overwhelming and unpleasant for them. Try leaving 8–10 drops of peppermint essential oil where you think they might be coming in, or in the corner of rooms, refreshing every few days. (Take care when using essential oils, however, if you have pets or young children around.)

. . . .

Dust mites

Regular cleaning helps to keep the dust mite population under control. Dust mites commonly live in house dust and feed on flakes of human skin. They thrive in

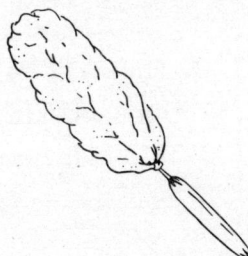

warm, centrally heated and carpeted homes, so it's a good idea to vacuum regularly and dust surfaces with a damp cloth or duster. Also wash your bed sheets once a week and air your house regularly. Dust mites – or rather the faeces they produce – is believed to be the most common cause of asthma, and they can cause eczema, itchy eyes, dermatitis and bronchitis as well. If you suffer from allergies, there are tips on page 248 for a cleaning routine especially tailored to you.

Fact check

What is dust?

Dust is made up of lots of components, including dead skin cells, hair, dust mites and fibres and fluff from carpets and clothes, as well as dirt, pollen and other particles from outside (often brought in on shoes).

QUICK FIVE-MINUTE CLEANS

When cleaning we often focus on certain areas of our homes, such as sinks, kitchen worktops and floors. But some areas can get overlooked, despite being places where germs and bacteria build up quickly, especially if they are touched by grimy hands every day. It takes just a few seconds or minutes to give them a quick clean, either with DIY disinfectant spray (see page 42) or with soapy water. Spend five minutes cleaning these forgotten areas:

Light switches
Door and cupboard handles
Top of kitchen cabinets
Doorknobs

Banisters and handrails

Skirting boards

Placemats

Remote controls and phones (see page 202)

Toothbrush holder

Bed bugs

Bed bugs are small parasitic insects, reddish-brown or yellow in colour and about the size of an apple seed when adult. They can hide in mattress seams, headboards and even curtains or wallpaper by day and are primarily active at night, causing itching and allergic reactions. Cleaning your bedding and mattress regularly will help prevent a breakout of bed bugs, but if you have an infestation, try the following methods:

- Wash bedding, along with curtains, clothing and any fabric items in your bedroom. Use a hot wash of at least 60°C (140°F) and add 10 drops of essential oil to the drawer – tea tree, lavender, eucalyptus, lemon, citronella, peppermint, cedarwood and clove oil are all known to repel or kill bed bugs. If you have a tumble dryer, dry on a hot setting for at least thirty minutes.
- You can also put any affected bedding and clothing in a plastic bag in the freezer for three or four days. Then put in a hot wash.
- Inspect the mattress and the bed frame regularly for any sign of bed bugs. Use a stiff brush to remove any bed bugs and eggs from seams before vacuuming.
- Deodorise your mattress with bicarbonate of soda and 10 drops of essential oil (see page 177).

- You can also spray the mattress, bed frames, headboard and other areas, including crevices and seams, with a DIY repellent spray made up of 60 ml (¼ cup) water, 10 drops of lavender essential oil and 10 drops of tea tree essential oil. Reapply the solution every day.
- Vacuum the mattress and area around it every day using an upholstery attachment. Avoid using the vacuum elsewhere in the house.
- If all else fails – and it is difficult to get rid of a beg bug infestation – contact a pest control service.

Pets

If you have pets, then your cleaning routine needs to factor them in, especially if muddy paws, litter trays and pet hair are a feature of your home. There's lots you can do to minimise the mess, including quick five-minute tasks and everyday habits.

- On a daily basis, brush your dog (and your cat if it will let you), removing any loose hairs in the process.
- Run a lint roller over chairs, cushions or wherever your pet settles – damp rubber gloves or dusting gloves will also work here. A good vacuum with an upholstery attachment will suck up pet hair, and a hand-held cordless vacuum will make this job even easier.
- Cover furniture you want to protect with washable throws and wash regularly.
- Set up a dog cleaning station close to where you enter your home. Here you could have old towels to wipe your dog down, or a tap or bowl of water to clean muddy paws. Put a mat down for you and your pet to

wipe their feet, and add some hooks nearby for leashes and other accessories.

- Wash pet bedding regularly. Remove any hair or fur, shake out any bits of mud, and then put in a washing machine or hand-wash or wipe down with a cloth. Bicarbonate of soda will neutralise odours; avoid any strongly scented products which may prove over-powering for your pet.

- Wash collars and leads seasonally or when needed, soaking them in hot soapy water or, if fabric, in a mesh garment bag in the washing machine.

- Wash toys when needed – you may find you need to do this regularly if your pet spends hours chewing and drooling on them. Plastic toys can go in the dishwasher, fabric ones in the washing machine.

- Put cat litter trays on a mat to catch any spilt litter. Change the litter regularly and scoop out clumps and waste at least once a day. Remove the litter and wash the tray once a week in soapy water and let dry. To prevent bad odours, add a layer of bicarbonate of soda before filling again.

- Always be careful when using cleaning products around pets as some are harmful to them. Natural products, such as bicarbonate of soda, tend to be safest.

. . . .

Top tips

To stop dogs peeing on the same part of a wall or gate outside your home: dogs don't like the smell of vinegar, so spray a solution of equal parts vinegar and water. You could also add 10–20 drops of peppermint oil, which acts as a deterrent, although ensure your dog doesn't ingest large amounts of it or gets it on to their skin. Spray for five days to a week and that should stop your dog peeing where it shouldn't.

You can also use a similar spray made up of equal parts vinegar and water to deter cats from scratching furniture. Add 20 drops of rosemary or lemon essential oil, both of which cats have a natural aversion to. Note that this solution could be toxic to cats so don't spray it on them, and make sure they don't lick it. Sometimes simply giving them a scratching post will entice them away from your furniture!

Stains

Spills and stains are all too common, from red wine and candle wax on carpets to splotches on clothes, fabrics or various surfaces around the home. When it comes to stains, speed is your friend, as the faster you can treat a stain, the better chance you'll have of removing it.

When you spot a stain, grab a clean cloth, sponge or tissue and try to absorb any excess liquid before it spreads. Always dab at the stain, and avoid rubbing, which can push the stain deeper into the fabric.

Top tip

Stains on clothes, such as coffee and drink spills and make-up marks, often happen when you're out and about. For that reason, I always make sure I have tissues and a hand sanitiser gel or liquid in my bag. The main ingredient in most hand sanitisers is alcohol, so it works well on coffee stains, pen marks, grease, make-up (including lipstick) and even grass stains. Blot any stains as soon as they happen and then apply the hand sanitiser, letting it sit for five minutes, before rubbing the area and then washing as normal when you get home. (Hand sanitiser gel is safe to use on many fabrics, but avoid on wool, rayon, silk or acetate.)

· ·

Here are a few quick removal techniques for various types of stains. Some will benefit from soaking to let a product work, but hands-on cleaning or preparation of solutions will take only a few minutes.

Grass

Remove any excess grass or mud, then saturate the stain with a solution of equal parts white vinegar and water and let it sit for five minutes. Apply laundry detergent, enough to cover the stain, massage it in for a few minutes, then let it sit for around ten to fifteen minutes. Rinse with cold water and the stain should have gone – if not, repeat the process.

Blood

Try to get to the stain as quickly as possible and flush it through with cold water. Apply hand or dish soap and gently work it in. Then rinse in cold water, apply more soap if necessary, rub it in and rinse again. If the stain is on clothing, wash as normal in your usual cycle. The process for removing blood stains from white sheets is very similar – flush out the stain as quickly as possible with cold water, then apply a little hydrogen peroxide (don't use this on coloured sheets), working it in with a soft brush, then wash as normal.

Grease and oil stains

Use a cloth or tissue to absorb as much oil and moisture as possible. Apply dish soap and work into the stain. Let it sit for ten minutes, then rinse with cold water and wash as normal. You can also sprinkle bicarbonate of soda on to the stain and leave for thirty minutes before washing.

Mud

Allow the mud to dry, then remove as much of it as possible, either by knocking off clumps or by using a blunt knife or toothbrush. Rub in some detergent and let it sit for fifteen minutes. Rub the stain with a toothbrush, loosening it from the fabric, and then wash on a normal cycle.

Suncream

Flush the stain with water and leave to dry. Squeeze lemon juice on to the stain, then pour salt on top. Let the juice and salt sit overnight, then brush off the salt and wash as normal.

Tomato or ketchup stains

Remove any food debris and soak up residue moisture. Mix equal parts white vinegar and warm water in a bowl, then add a few drops of dish soap. Apply to the stain, gently scrubbing with a soft brush or damp cloth. Let it sit for at least fifteen minutes, then wash the item in cold water. That will hopefully be enough to remove the stain, but if it won't budge you could also try mixing a paste of two parts bicarbonate of soda and one part water. Apply to the affected area and work into the stain with a toothbrush.

Red wine

Soak up any excess wine as quickly as possible. Fill a bowl with warm water, a drop of white vinegar and a squirt of dish soap and apply to the stain. Let it sit for a few minutes then blot dry with a clean cloth. If the natural method doesn't work, then I might use a Dr. Beckmann stain remover on my carpets, followed by a steam clean which can also lift and loosen stains and dirt.

Ink

It can be really tough getting pen or ink marks out of clothing or fabric. The best way to remove them is to soak the mark or stain in rubbing alcohol for fifteen minutes, then rinse in cold water.

Nail polish

Dab on a very small amount of rubbing alcohol or non-oily nail polish remover.

Candle wax

Let the wax cool and then scrape off with a blunt knife. You can also lay a clean cloth or paper towel over the wax and press down gently with a warm (but not very hot) iron. The heat should cause the wax to transfer on to the cloth. When removing hardened wax from crevices or grooves, use your hair dryer on a medium setting, direct it at the wax and then wipe away the softened wax.

Wall marks

Rubbing with a tennis ball will remove many wall marks. Warm soapy water will usually remove handprints on walls, or try wiping them off with a chunk of stale white bread dampened with a little water. For crayon marks, apply some bicarbonate of soda, vinegar or even toothpaste to an old toothbrush and scrub the spot. If all else fails, you could try using a magic eraser, but always test on an inconspicuous area first if using on a painted wall.

Water rings

Act quickly, and if it's waxed wood you can try rubbing on a little rubbing alcohol (although test on an inconspicuous area first).

Stickers

For sticker residues on walls or doors (kids love a sticker!), add a very small amount of nail polish remover or surgical spirit, rub gently and it should come away easily.

Tupperware

For recent stains, fill with warm water and a few squirts of dish soap. Tear up some pieces of paper towel, add to the soapy mixture, seal the Tupperware tightly and shake for a minute or two. You can also make a paste of bicarbonate of soda and water, spread it all over, leave for an hour or two and rinse.

Fake tan

Mix equal parts bicarbonate of soda and cold water to create a paste. Apply it to the stain, leave for fifteen minutes and wash off with cold or warm water. For fake tan stains on surfaces like toilet seats – more common than you think! – you could also try rubbing with a magic eraser.

Lipstick

Dab nail polish remover or white vinegar on to the stain, then brush lightly with a toothbrush. Rinse out with rubbing alcohol and wash as normal.

· ·

Pushchairs and highchairs

If you have young children, you'll know just how grubby pushchairs, prams and highchairs can get. Prams are out in all weather, while crumbs, food and drink spills can accumulate in buggies and highchairs, making them a hotspot for germs. Give them a good clean monthly or seasonally, depending on use.

- On a daily or weekly basis, you can do a quick five-minute blitz, tipping the pushchair upside down and shaking out any crumbs or dried on dirt. You can also give it a quick vacuum, using an attachment for crevices and seams. Give the seat and hood a wash with soapy water. Do the same with a highchair, wiping down the frame, legs and tray top with a DIY disinfectant spray (see page 42) or soapy water and allow to dry.
- For more of a deep-clean, if the pushchair or highchair has a removable fabric seat or hood, remove and put it in the washing machine, or hand-wash according to the

care label. If the fabric seat cannot be removed, steam clean the fabric or wipe it down with soapy water or DIY disinfectant spray.

- Any stains or ground-in food might need more of a scrub, perhaps with a paste of bicarbonate of soda and water, which will help to lift it and also neutralise odours from milk or urine spills. Leave to dry.

Allergy cleaning routine

If you or people you live with suffer from allergies, or from conditions such as asthma or eczema, you may need to tailor your cleaning routine accordingly. Dust and some cleaning products can cause wheezing, skin irritation and general allergic reactions, so here are a few tips.

- Some cleaning products contain harsh chemicals, so it's best to stick to natural products such as bicarbonate of soda and vinegar. That way you avoid breathing in toxic chemicals and smells.
- Wear protective gloves when cleaning – rubber, latex or PVC if you're not sensitive to them, or cotton gloves if you are.
- You could also wear a face mask when cleaning, changing beds, vacuuming and dusting.
- Ventilate the room – throw open the windows – when cleaning.
- Vacuum at least twice a week and pay attention to edges of carpets, under furniture and beds. Make sure your vacuum has a HEPA (high-efficiency particulate

air filter), which removes minute dust particles, and change the filter frequently.

- To trap dust rather than send it airborne, dust with a dampened duster using DIY dusting spray (page 36).
- Keep surfaces dust free and cut down on ornaments.
- Dust and mop skirting boards and walls regularly.
- Dust/vacuum or steam clean upholstery and curtains regularly.
- After cleaning, wash your hands in warm soapy water or take a shower to remove dust from hair and skin, and change your clothes.

If you have a severe allergy to dust, it's advisable to have hard floors (wooden, laminate etc.) and a few rugs rather than extensive carpeting. On average, a house with hard floors and a few rugs will have a tenth of the dust in a house fitted with wall-to-wall carpets.

The unpleasant stuff

Okay, now the unpleasant stuff, and we're talking human emissions here, not those from pets! Arm yourself with a sturdy pair of cleaning gloves before tackling any of the stains below.

Vomit

Scrape up as much as you can with tissue and a blunt knife. Sprinkle over a generous layer of bicarbonate of soda, which will help neutralise the smell. Leave it for fifteen minutes and vacuum, finishing with some DIY fabric refresher spray (see page 258). Scrub any stain with warm water and a splash of white vinegar. Blot dry.

Urine

For urine stains on mattresses or any fabric – absorb as much excess urine as possible with an old towel or paper towels. Mix equal parts vinegar and warm water, then add 1 tablespoon of bicarbonate of soda for every cup of liquid. Mix thoroughly, then spray the solution on to the soiled area, wait ten minutes, and blot it up with paper towels or a cloth. You can also use shaving foam in the same way.

Faeces

Get yourself lots of kitchen tissue, scoop up and remove the mess, then try to absorb any remaining excess moisture. Once that's done, spray on equal parts white vinegar and water. Scrub with an old toothbrush (then throw it away) and blot the area again with paper towels. When dry, sprinkle over a layer of bicarbonate of soda and a drop of essential oil, leave for ten minutes and vacuum up.

NOTES

....

....

....

....

....

....

....

....

....

....

CHECKLIST

.... ☐

.... ☐

.... ☐

.... ☐

.... ☐

.... ☐

.... ☐

.... ☐

.... ☐

.... ☐

.... ☐

.... ☐

.... ☐

.... ☐

.... ☐

.... ☐

.... ☐

.... ☐

.... ☐

.... ☐

.... ☐

.... ☐

.... ☐

.... ☐

.... ☐

.... ☐

.... ☐

MONDAY

TUESDAY

WEDNESDAY

THURSDAY

FRIDAY

SATURDAY

SUNDAY

CHAPTER 11

SPECIAL TOUCHES

Maintaining a clean home can be rewarding, but adding a few special touches can truly make it feel like your own. I love to fill my home with mood-boosting fragrances, from fresh floral scents to woody cinnamon aromas, and here are lots of simple ideas on how to do that, without buying expensive products. I've also included tips on elements you can add when guests come to stay, as well as a seven-day cleaning countdown for Christmas and other seasonal celebrations to help you stay in control and get ready for those special occasions.

QUICK CLEANING TIPS

- Do what's easy and requires the least maintenance
- Before a big occasion, make a list
- Clean gradually and don't leave preparations until the last minute
- Don't expect perfection when guests stay
- Above all, enjoy your home and focus on what you love

Fragrances

Cleaning your home regularly will prevent many odours, especially if you clean your toilet thoroughly, empty and clean your bins and change your bed sheets. As you'll know by now, vinegar and bicarbonate of soda are your friends when it comes to neutralising smells, but sometimes adding a few natural fragrances around the home can uplift your spirits and make a home feel inviting. Here are a few easy-to-make, chemical-free options.

Air freshener

Make your own air freshener by filling a spray bottle with warm water and 10 drops of your favourite essential oils (see page 43). If your goal is to neutralise odours in the home, remove bacteria and generally disinfect the air, you could also fill a spray bottle with one part white vinegar to four parts water.

Fabric refresher

Spritz your carpets, curtains and fabrics with this DIY spray. Carefully fill a spray bottle with boiling water, add 2 teaspoons of bicarbonate of soda and 10 drops of essential oil. Shake and leave for thirty minutes to diffuse.

Coffee bean candle

This is a great way to get rid of unwanted odours in the home as well as cooking smells in the kitchen! All you have to do is fill a ramekin with coffee beans and place an unscented tea light in the centre of the beans. Burning the candle will heat the coffee beans so they give off a lovely aroma.

Wax melt

Wax melts add fragrance to your home for long periods. They are made up of blocks of scented wax which melt when heated in a wax burner, releasing their aroma. There are a wide variety of different scents, meaning you can choose a new aroma every day. They are also really affordable and contain less wax than many candles.

Reed diffuser

Reed diffusers can be quite pricey, and many of the cheaper ones release artificial scents. However it's easy to make up your own and to choose a natural scent or mixture of aromas that you love!

A small glass or ceramic vase or bottle with a
    narrow opening at the top (so the oil evaporates
    more slowly)
Diffuser reeds (or trimmed bamboo skewers)
Mineral oil for the base – typically sweet almond oil
Your favourite essential oils – I like rosemary, eucalyptus and
    lemon, but the choice is yours (just remember that some
    oils are unsuitable for pets and pregnant women)

Pour 60 ml (¼ cup) almond oil into the base of your bottle or vase. Add around 30 drops of essential oil and give it a good shake to mix the oils. Put in 5–8 reeds and flip them after one hour. Flip them once a week and replace the oil once a month for a continuous scent.

You may need to alter the amounts depending on the size of your bottle.

Plants, flowers and herbs

Plants not only have a calming effect, but they also purify the air, absorb toxins, keep your home smelling fresh and add a touch of beauty, texture and focus to a room. They can also help to remove excess moisture, reducing condensation and mould growth in typically damp and steamy areas like bathrooms. When choosing plants for a bathroom, go for ones that can cope with humid conditions, such as aloe vera, spider plants, snake plants, peace lilies and ferns.

A vase full of flowers is another mood-booster, adding colour and fragrance to any room. Roses, sweet peas, lilacs, hyacinths (which you can grow indoors), lilies and geraniums give off a wonderful perfume and of course look beautiful. Freshly snipped herbs, such as rosemary, lavender and mint, can also fill a house with natural scent, and a simple posy in a bud vase can look pretty.

Top tips

- Keep freshly picked lavender in a vase by your bed to help you drift off to sleep. Dried lavender can be hung in wardrobes or kept in a scent bag to line drawers (see page 262), and makes a great end-of-year teacher's present!
- To dry lavender, hang bundles of it upside down in a warm, dry place, although avoid direct sunlight as this will fade the colour. The drying process will take seven to ten days.
- Nicotiana (tobacco plant) comes alive at night. Fill a vase with it and put it in your bedroom for a rich jasmine-like scent as you fall asleep.

EUCALYPTUS

If you want to add a spa-like touch to your bathroom, hang up or put in a vase some dried or fresh eucalyptus stems. If you use fresh eucalyptus, crush the leaves a little with a rolling pin before tying into a bundle so they release their aroma.

The steam from your bath or shower will release the eucalyptus oils into the air, which have a calming effect, act as a natural decongestant, can help fight off infections, boost circulation, relieve pain and even stimulate your mind – it really is a miracle plant! Some people even hang stems

just behind their shower head, so they get the full effect of the steam. Fresh eucalyptus will usually last about a month and dried eucalyptus about three months, depending on the humidity in your bathroom.

Scent bags

Another DIY project which uses all-natural products are scent bags made from dried herbs, dried flowers or dried fruit peel. They are perfect for placing in drawers and closets all around your home, and especially in guest rooms; you could also pop them in cushions, storage boxes containing clothes, and even in the car. They also make lovely gifts and you can vary the contents according to your preference and mood.

Organza bags (shop-bought) with a drawstring
Dried herbs, flowers or peel, such as lavender, rose petals, camomile, lemon peel, mint (see the various blends suggested below, but you could experiment here)
Essential oils of your choice
Absorbent agent, e.g. rice, Epsom salt or bicarbonate of soda (this holds the fragrance and absorbs any moisture)

In a bowl, mix one part herbs or flowers with two parts absorbent agent. Add a few drops of essential oil to enhance the scent and mix thoroughly. Fill each organza bag about three-quarters full, allowing a little space so you can close it comfortably. Tie securely in a knot or bow.

Suggested blends for different scents:

- Energising – dried rosemary, dried peppermint leaves, lemon peel, Epsom salt or rice, essential oils: lemon, peppermint

- Calming – dried lavender, chamomile, Epsom salt, essential oils: lavender, chamomile
- Refreshing citrus – dried lemon peel, dried orange peel, mint leaves, Epsom salt, essential oils: orange, lemon, peppermint
- Cosy autumnal night – dried cinnamon sticks (broken into small pieces), dried cloves, dried orange peel, rice or bicarbonate of soda, essential oils: cinnamon, clove, orange, nutmeg
- Floral blend – dried rose petals, dried lavender, dried jasmine, bicarbonate of soda, essential oils: rose, jasmine, lavender
- Christmas blend – orange peel, cinnamon sticks, cloves, bay leaves, rice or Epsom salt, essential oils: cinnamon, clove, orange, pine. For a festive touch add a small bell, ribbon or rosemary sprig

Pomander balls

Making pomander balls, a traditional Christmas craft, will fill your home with festive scents. Typically, they are made from fresh oranges, but you can make them with lemons, limes or other citrus fruits, which are then studded with cloves. You can prick holes for the cloves with a cocktail stick, then insert the pointed end of each clove, creating a pattern of diamonds, circles or swirls. For extra fragrance you can roll the finished fruit in a mixture of ground spices like nutmeg or cinnamon – this enhances the scent and preserves the fruit. Wrap a ribbon around the fruit, leaving space for a hanging loop. Place it in a cool, dry place for about two weeks, turning it occasionally, and as it dries it will release lovely aromas. Once dry you can hang it on your Christmas tree, in a window or place it in a decorative bowl.

Tips for ways to keep your home smelling fresh

- Add a few drops of essential oil to cotton wool balls and place in the base of a bin to keep it smelling fresh.
- Deodorise your carpets using bicarbonate of soda and sweet orange essential oil. Sprinkle over your carpets/rugs and vacuum up after fifteen minutes. This will rid them of nasty odours, leaving them with a lovely scent!
- If you have a damp, mouldy smell in a room, a short-term quick fix is to place a bowl of bicarbonate of soda in the room to soak up any moisture and bad smells. (See page 130 for how to remove mould and mildew.)
- Lingering cooking smells? Place a bowl of apple cider or distilled white vinegar in your kitchen to absorb the odour. Or add one or two capfuls of your favourite disinfectant to a kitchen sink filled with boiling water – the steam will fill the room. If you have particularly fishy smells, combine 480 ml (2 cups) water, 3 tablespoons bicarbonate of soda, and some lemon peel in a bowl and leave overnight in the kitchen.
- Smelly trainers? Add dry tea bags and leave under a radiator or in a warm airing cupboard. Or sprinkle in a layer of bicarbonate of soda, tipping out before you wear them. Spray with fabric refresher (see page 258) or dry shampoo after wearing.

Simmer pots

Another way to waft inviting aromas throughout your home is to have simmer pots bubbling on your stove. Just fill a large saucepan of water with seasonal herbs, fruits and spices, and let it simmer away for a few hours. Your home will smell amazing. Here are a few variations, which will infuse your home with wonderful seasonal smells.

· ·

CHRISTMAS SIMMER POT

250 g (1 cup) fresh cranberries
1 whole orange (with peel), sliced
1 teaspoon vanilla extract
1 teaspoon cloves
1 cinnamon stick
2 sprigs of rosemary

Fill a saucepan with water and bring to the boil. Add the ingredients, continue to boil for a minute or two, then turn the heat down and bring to a simmer, without the lid. You can leave this to simmer away for hours by topping up with water when needed, and it will also last for up to four days if you want to reuse it! You can keep it in the fridge in between uses and I have also used the leftover water as a DIY air freshener too.

· ·

AUTUMN SIMMER POT

1 whole orange (with peel), sliced
1 whole apple, sliced

1 teaspoon vanilla extract
1 teaspoon cloves
1 cinnamon stick

Follow the instructions for the Christmas simmer pot (see page 265).

. . . .

SPRING AND SUMMER SIMMER POT

1 whole lemon (with peel), sliced
2 sprigs of rosemary
1 teaspoon cloves
1 tablespoon vanilla extract

Follow the instructions for the Christmas simmer pot (see page 265).

. . . .

HERBAL SIMMER POT

4 basil leaves
2 sprigs of rosemary
2 sprigs of parsley
4 mint leaves

Follow the instructions for the Christmas simmer pot (see page 265).

Guests

When guests are staying, there are lots of special touches you can add to make your home feel comfortable and inviting.

If you have guests arriving with little or no warning – we've all been there! – here's a quick run-down of what you can do in five to fifteen minutes of cleaning and tidying.

- Tidy away clutter.
- Put dirty dishes in the dishwasher or spend a couple of minutes washing up.
- Wipe the kitchen worktops and clean up any food spills.
- Plump up cushions on sofas and chairs.
- Do a quick vacuum.
- Spray some air freshener.
- Answer the door!

If you have a bit more time, here's what you might need to do to prepare a bedroom for a guest, whether they are in your spare room or you're repurposing another bedroom. If your time is limited you can do these jobs gradually over a few days.

- Vacuum the floor, sprinkling with some bicarbonate of soda or essential oil if needed.
- Dust hard surfaces.
- Open the window. If the room hasn't been used for a while, it might smell a little musty. Give the blind, shutter or curtain a dust or wipe.
- Clean the windows (see page 86) and polish any mirrors.
- Clear out anything lurking underneath the bed.
- Add a bunch of flowers, herbs or a plant or a reed diffuser.

- Change the bed linen so it's clean and fresh, and give the headboard and frame a wipe. Add a couple of blankets and extra cushions.
- Put some fresh towels in the room, or some basic toiletries and a box of tissues.
- Empty and change any bins, adding some essential oil in the base.
- Make space in a wardrobe or in a chest of drawers, spray a little air or fabric freshener in the wardrobe and add a scent bag (see page 262).
- Put a bottle or carafe of water and glass by the bed-side table.
- Make sure the bedside lamp works and leave a note with the wifi code.

Festive clean routine

Preparing your home so it's a festive, inviting space for friends and family can be great fun but also a little daunting. Break the tasks down into manageable five-minute chunks, do them over a week and you'll ensure your home is clean, organised and looking suitably festive for the holiday season. This can apply to Christmas or any seasonal celebration or occasion when you're welcoming friends and family into your home.

The following cleaning routine covers the week before Christmas or your seasonal celebration, but you can of course spread this over a month, especially if you like to get your Christmas decorations up a few weeks before the big day! Some of these tasks, such as deep-cleaning the sofa or cleaning windows, will take longer than five minutes, so don't feel you have to do everything on the list. Choose what is realistic and manageable for you.

Seven days before – Declutter and organise

- Remove clutter and unwanted items from living room and communal areas so they are ready for Christmas decorations
- Create some closet and drawer space in guest bedroom/s
- Remove coats, shoes or unnecessary items in entrance way
- Remove expired food items in kitchen, creating space in the fridge and cupboards for more food

Six days before – Deep-clean living areas

- Clean windows and mirrors
- Deep-clean sofa and chairs
- Wash cushions or any throws
- Deodorise carpets and floors

Five days before – Deep-clean kitchen

- Wipe down worktops, outside of cabinets and splashbacks
- Deep-clean kettle, toaster or regularly used appliances
- Wipe down shelves and inside of fridge
- Clean windows

Four days before – Clean guest bedroom/s

- Change bed linen, dust and vacuum room
- Add plant, diffuser, fresh towels
- Make sure bedside lamp works

Three days before – Seasonal touches

- Put up Christmas decorations, tree and wreath, if not already done
- Fill your house with fragrances – dried herbs, flowers, or prepare a Christmas simmer pot
- Stock up on holiday snacks and drinks

Two days before – Deep-clean bathrooms

- Deep-clean toilet, removing any stains
- Scrub shower, bath, sinks
- Clean mirrors, windows and counters
- Mop floor and change bins

One day before – Final touches

- Vacuum entrance way and living area
- Dust hard surfaces
- Wipe downs kitchen tops, change bins
- Put fresh towels and water/glass in guest bedrooms
- Ensure there's plenty of soap, toilet paper and fresh towels in bathrooms

Then congratulate yourself, put your feet up and enjoy the big day!

NOTES

CHECKLIST

.... ☐

.... ☐

.... ☐

.... ☐

.... ☐

.... ☐

.... ☐

.... ☐

.... ☐

.... ☐

.... ☐

.... ☐

SPECIAL TOUCHES

.... ☐

.... ☐

.... ☐

.... ☐

.... ☐

.... ☐

.... ☐

.... ☐

.... ☐

.... ☐

.... ☐

.... ☐

.... ☐

.... ☐

.... ☐

MONDAY

TUESDAY

WEDNESDAY

THURSDAY

FRIDAY

SATURDAY

SUNDAY

CHAPTER 12

CREATE YOUR OWN
FIVE-MINUTE CLEAN ROUTINE

This chapter provides detailed cleaning routines as well as space for you to create your own thirty-day planner. It's entirely your call whether you try out one of the options provided here, build your own, or just go with the flow. I'll remind you of some of the routines covered in earlier chapters, just to encapsulate how you might kick-start a new plan, and then move on to a sample monthly planner, which you can revise as you go along. I've also included a thirty-day declutter challenge and a spring-clean and clear challenge.

At its heart, the Five-Minute Clean Routine is made up of quick cleaning tasks, some of which are everyday habits and chores, and some of which you do on a weekly, monthly or seasonal basis. First, repeat those everyday cleaning habits so they become automatic and part of the natural flow of your day. Here's a reminder of what these habits could encompass.

QUICK CLEANING TIPS

- Take items with you when you leave a room
- Pick up what you drop
- Clean up any mess or spillages as soon as they happen
- Wash dishes and clear up after meals
- Deal with stuff coming into the house

And here's a reminder of what those habitual tasks might look like during the day.

MORNING

Make bed and reset bedroom
Wipe down sink and surfaces in bathroom
Put away dishes from dishwasher or draining board
Clean away breakfast things
Put on a load of washing

LUNCHTIME (IF HOME)

Hang up or fold laundry
Give toilets a freshen up
Go through post

EVENING

Soak pots as you eat
Clear away and wash or load dinner things
Wipe dining table, worktops and hob
Quick sweep or vacuum of floor
Reset living room before bed

You can then start to combine these daily habits with other five-minute cleaning tasks, choosing from those outlined in the checklists at the end of every room chapter. You might focus on a certain room, giving each one a deep-clean over one week, or different areas of your home, such as the beds or windows.

Some tasks will take longer than five minutes, and you can break these down into smaller chunks of cleaning or tackle them when you have the time or are in the mood. The planner on pages 280–285 includes a variety of tasks, including optional monthly or seasonal deep-cleans that might require a little more of your time.

In devising a cleaning routine you should also consider when you can fit in your five-minute cleans (or longer deep-cleans). Do you have more time and energy in the morning? Is it best to do some cleaning before you relax in the evening, or as part of a house reset last thing at night? Can you get in a quick five to ten minutes of cleaning before you pick up your kids or attend a work meeting? Have you factored in time for exercise, rest, reading, gardening, or whatever it is that helps with your emotional wellbeing?

Make a note of all your fixed commitments and activities in a typical week, then write down time spent doing other things: making meals, getting dressed, on your phone/social media or messaging, shopping, watching TV, etc. Journal everything you do as you do it, so you get a realistic idea of the general framework of your day and when you can fit in those bouts of cleaning. I bet, like me, you could easily cut down on some of that screen and scrolling time, replacing it with ticking off the odd cleaning task.

Four-week planner

This four-week planner is largely made up of weekly and monthly tasks, plus optional monthly or seasonal jobs, which are likely to take more than five minutes so you should tackle them only when you have the time or energy. It's a more detailed version of the planner first outlined in chapter three. Each week focuses on giving one room – bathroom, kitchen, bedroom, living area – a thorough clean. Every day there is a five-minute task for that room, alongside two other five-minute tasks elsewhere in the home. Remember to utilise all the tips I've outlined to speed up your cleaning.

This is not a definitive list of tasks – you may want to add, take away or revise the planner as you do it, according to what works best for you, your lifestyle and your home.

WEEK 1 – FOCUS ON BATHROOM

Monday – Deep-clean toilet and disinfect toilet brush

- Wipe down and empty kitchen bins
- Wipe kitchen sink, taps and splashbacks

Tuesday – Clean shower/screen or bath and surrounding tiles/surfaces

- Vacuum living area
- Dust hard surfaces in living area

Wednesday – Clean sink, taps and mirrors

- Clean mirrors in bedroom and living areas
- Rinse out dishwasher filter

Thursday – Mop floor and walls

- Mop kitchen floor
- Vacuum bedroom/s

Friday – Wash towels, mats and shower curtain

- Clean fridge surfaces
- Dust hard surfaces in bedroom/s

Saturday – Flush out plug holes, wipe cupboards and surfaces

- Clean window/s in kitchen or living area
- Wipe down kitchen cupboards

Sunday – Disinfect toothbrush, empty and wipe bins

- Change and wash bedding
- Do ironing

Optional Monthly/Seasonal Bathroom Tasks: deep-clean radiators, whiten tile grouting, descale shower head, declutter toiletries, clean extractor fan/vent, clean windows

WEEK 2 – FOCUS ON BEDROOM

Monday – Dust hard surfaces and lampshades

- Clean kitchen sink and taps
- Declutter and clean one kitchen cupboard

Tuesday – Dust blinds/curtains and headboard

- Run empty hot wash or self-cleaning wash in washing machine
- Deep-clean toilet

Wednesday – Sort/clean make-up brushes and products

- Vacuum living area and entrance way
- Dust hard surfaces and work area in living area

Thursday – Vacuum, sweep or mop floors

- Wipe down kitchen bins
- Mop and clean shower or bath

Friday – Sort through and declutter clothing

- Clean mirrors and surfaces in bathroom
- Clean inside fridge

Saturday – Clean windows

- Wipe down kitchen bins and rinse out dishwasher filter
- Mop kitchen floor

Sunday – Change bedding and vacuum/deodorise mattress

- Vacuum sofa and chairs
- Wash bathroom towels and mat

Optional Monthly/Seasonal Bedroom Tasks: dust/mop walls, dust light fixtures/fans, wash duvets and pillows, wash hairbrush

WEEK 3 – FOCUS ON KITCHEN

Monday – Clean sink, taps and hob

- Mop bathroom floor
- Clean bedroom and bathroom mirrors

Tuesday – Mop floor, wipe down tiles and splashbacks

- Deep-clean toilet
- Wipe bathroom surfaces and empty bin

Wednesday – Clean and declutter fridge

- Dust and tidy workspace
- Dust hard surfaces in living area

Thursday – Clean windows

- Vacuum living area
- Vacuum bedroom

Friday – Descale kettle, clean chopping board and microwave

- Wash make-up brush and sponges
- Dust blinds and curtains in living area

Saturday – Flush out plug holes, declutter one cupboard

- Clean shower or bath
- Wash bath towels and mat

Sunday – Give pots/pans a clean, clean coffee machine or toaster

- Vacuum sofa and chairs
- Change and wash bedding

Optional Monthly/Seasonal Kitchen Tasks: mop walls and dust light fixtures, clean cooker hood, clean oven, deep-clean hob

WEEK 4 - FOCUS ON LIVING AREAS

Monday - Vacuum floors and mop skirting boards

- Mop kitchen floor
- Mop bathroom floor

Tuesday - Clean windows

- Deep-clean toilet
- Clean bathroom sink and taps

Wednesday - Dust and mop walls, dust ceiling lights/fans

- Dust office space
- Disinfect phone and electrical equipment

Thursday - Deep-clean sofas and chairs

- Vacuum bedroom
- Clean kitchen sinks and splashbacks

Friday - Dust surfaces and workspace, clean and disinfect phones/computer equipment

- Wipe down kitchen bins
- Clean bedroom and bathroom mirrors

Saturday – Clean stairs, entrance way and spot clean carpet stains

- Wash out filter on tumble dryer or clean iron soleplate
- Clean shower screen or bath

Sunday – Dust blinds or vacuum/steam curtains

- Wash and change bedding
- Wash make up brush and sponges

Optional Monthly/Seasonal Living Area Tasks: steam clean carpets, deodorise rugs and carpets, wash sofa cover, clean radiators, clean curtains.

. . . .

Once you've mapped out the rooms and tasks you want to cover, you can then work up your own monthly planner. You could print it out and put it somewhere visible at home, in a cleaning caddy or keep it on your phone, perhaps with prompts in your calendar, treating your five-minute cleaning jobs like appointments in your day.

Remember, your cleaning planner is not set in stone – the first month of cleaning is a trial run and you can revise it as you go. You might find you've inadvertently left out a key cleaning task or you've allocated too much or too little time to certain jobs. Cleaning is an ongoing process; it doesn't happen overnight and there might be days when you can't clean and days when you're raring to go. If the planner doesn't work out, remember that it's not you that's failed, it's the planner, so revise it and work out what is feasible for you.

Declutter challenge

If you feel you need to declutter your home before you embark on your new cleaning routine, give this thirty-day declutter challenge a go. Set a time and give yourself five minutes a day – it's amazing how much you can get done! Some jobs will take longer than five minutes so you may need to do them over a few days – or keep going if you're in the mood for it. You can also refer to chapter four for tips on decluttering.

- Walk around home with a 'throw it away' bag
- Walk around home with a 'donate it' bag
- Declutter cleaning products and tools
- Empty and declutter junk drawer
- Test and declutter electrical items, such as torches
- Sort through junk mail
- Go through food cupboard and throw out items past expiry date
- Sort through tea towels
- Go through coats and other items in entrance way
- Assess and pare down decorative items in living area
- Declutter fridge
- Go through and file important documents
- Declutter instruction manuals
- Declutter handbag or wallet
- Throw out chipped kitchen mugs
- Declutter kitchen glasses
- Declutter toys and books
- Minimise bedding
- Sort through bathroom towels, mats and flannels
- Empty and declutter storage cupboard
- Declutter Tupperware

- Sort through kitchen appliances
- Declutter kitchen utensils
- Find books to donate
- Declutter bathroom toiletries
- Sort through one clothes drawer in bedroom
- Declutter one area of wardrobe
- Sort through accessories in bedroom
- Declutter underwear and socks
- Organise and declutter desk area

Spring clean and clear challenge

If you're feeling really motivated, here's a spring clean and clear challenge. It includes some of those seasonal deep-cleans for days when you have a bit more time, as well as quick five-minute jobs for areas often forgotten around the house. Combine this with your usual cleaning routine. You don't have to do this in the spring – you might find the beginning of the year is a better time for you, or the end of the summer, or whenever you have the time. You could also spread this over six weeks, three months, whatever works for you!

- Declutter and clean fridge
- Wipe and disinfect light switches and door handles
- Dust picture frames and tops of doors
- Deep-clean dishwasher
- Clean extractor fan filters
- Descale kettle
- Deep-clean oven
- Dust and mop walls
- Deep-clean kitchen worktops and splashbacks
- Dust ceiling light fixtures

- Dust or mop skirting boards
- Deodorise and turn mattress
- Deep-clean kitchen hob
- Clean cooker hood
- Wipe down kitchen cabinets
- Wipe and polish banisters
- Dust/wash/steam curtains or blinds
- Clean windows
- Clean radiators
- Clean window frames and runners
- Whiten grouting in bathroom or kitchen
- Deep-clean washing machine
- Wash or steam clean carpets
- Wash duvets and pillows
- Remove mould or mildew in bathroom
- Clean and declutter make-up
- Whiten toilet bowl
- Disinfect remote controls and phones
- Clean toaster, coffee maker or kitchen appliance
- Wash pet accessories

CONCLUSION

So there you have it – the Five-Minute Clean Routine! Develop those daily cleaning habits, throw in a few extra five-minute tasks every day, add the odd deep-clean and you'll have a cleaner, more organised home.

Remember to start small: see how much you can achieve in five minutes and take it from there. Tick off those five-minute jobs, treat them as small wins, and you might feel like carrying on! And remember: developing any new routine takes time. You'll need to work it in around your other commitments and figure out what's realistic for you and the people you live with.

Whatever happens, keep motivated – play some music when you clean, tick another item off that to-do list, or breathe in the fresh scents of essential oils. Keep reminding yourself of your achievements. I'd love to hear how you're doing, and if you want to share your progress or pass on any tips or favourite gadgets – feel free (@anna_louisa_at_home)!

Whatever your needs are when it comes to cleaning, I hope this book provides some inspiration and a few ideas, and shows that you can fit in quick bursts of cleaning to suit your mood or schedule. I also hope you enjoy some of these tasks and the results they bring – I know keeping a clean home keeps me calm and grounded. Lastly, a big thank you for buying the book – it's been such fun to write and to bring together all the tips I've learnt along the way, and an honour to pass them on to you now.

So, give the routine a go and discover just how much you can achieve in five minutes!

Anna Louisa

NOTES

NOTES

NOTES

CHECKLIST

.... ☐

.... ☐

.... ☐

.... ☐

.... ☐

.... ☐

.... ☐

.... ☐

.... ☐

.... ☐

.... ☐

.... ☐

CHECKLIST

.... ☐

.... ☐

.... ☐

.... ☐

.... ☐

.... ☐

.... ☐

.... ☐

.... ☐

.... ☐

.... ☐

.... ☐

.... ☐

.... ☐

.... ☐

CHECKLIST

.... ☐

.... ☐

.... ☐

.... ☐

.... ☐

.... ☐

.... ☐

.... ☐

.... ☐

.... ☐

.... ☐

.... ☐

.... ☐

.... ☐

.... ☐

.... ☐

CHECKLIST

.... ☐

.... ☐

.... ☐

.... ☐

.... ☐

.... ☐

.... ☐

.... ☐

.... ☐

.... ☐

.... ☐

.... ☐

.... ☐

.... ☐

.... ☐

.... ☐

CHECKLIST

.... ☐

.... ☐

.... ☐

.... ☐

.... ☐

.... ☐

.... ☐

.... ☐

.... ☐

.... ☐

.... ☐

.... ☐

.... ☐

.... ☐

.... ☐

CHECKLIST

.... ☐

.... ☐

.... ☐

.... ☐

.... ☐

.... ☐

.... ☐

.... ☐

.... ☐

.... ☐

.... ☐

.... ☐

.... ☐

.... ☐

.... ☐

MONDAY

TUESDAY

WEDNESDAY

THURSDAY

FRIDAY

SATURDAY

SUNDAY

MONDAY

TUESDAY

WEDNESDAY

THURSDAY

FRIDAY

SATURDAY

SUNDAY

MONDAY

TUESDAY

WEDNESDAY

THURSDAY

FRIDAY

SATURDAY

SUNDAY

MONDAY

TUESDAY

WEDNESDAY

THURSDAY

FRIDAY

SATURDAY

SUNDAY

MONDAY

TUESDAY

WEDNESDAY

THURSDAY

FRIDAY

SATURDAY

SUNDAY

MONDAY

TUESDAY

WEDNESDAY

THURSDAY

FRIDAY

SATURDAY

SUNDAY

MONDAY

TUESDAY

WEDNESDAY

THURSDAY

FRIDAY

SATURDAY

SUNDAY

ACKNOWLEDGEMENTS

Wow. What a moment. Writing these acknowledgements feels surreal. To hold this book in my hands, and to know it's out there in the world, is a dream I never dared to believe could come true.

First and foremost, I have to thank *you*, my incredible followers. You've been there from the very beginning, cheering me on through every cleaning hack, every tip shared, and every moment of chaos and calm. Your messages, comments and support have meant the world to me, and this book wouldn't exist without your encouragement. You are the heart of this journey, and I'm endlessly grateful to each and every one of you.

A huge thank you to the amazing Emma Marriott and the team at Century. Your belief in me, your guidance and your hard work have made this book shine brighter than I ever could have imagined. Thank you for taking a chance on me and for walking me through every step of this new, exciting adventure.

To my incredible team at Outreach Talent Group, with a special shout-out to my manager and friend Rosie Adams: thank you for keeping me calm, inspired and focused. Your unwavering support has been invaluable, and I feel so lucky to have you in my corner.

To my amazing husband, family and friends – thank you for being my rock. For always cheering me on, for tolerating my endless cleaning experiments, and for reminding me to take breaks when I got carried away. Your love has been my anchor through it all.

This book is more than just words on a page – it's a piece of my heart. It's for anyone who's ever felt overwhelmed, for anyone who's struggled to find balance, and for anyone who just needs a little help to feel at home. Thank you for being part of this dream.

Here's to the start of something truly magical.

With all my love and gratitude,
Anna Louisa x

INDEX

abrasive cleaning products 49, 51, 52, 127, 129, 148, 160, 164, 202

ADHD, autism or neurodivergent conditions 13, 91

air freshener 46, 258

air fryer 158

all-purpose cleaner 33, 35, 36, 44, 46, 50, 57, 106, 107, 108, 109, 132, 138, 148, 234

allergies 22, 24, 60, 61, 128, 175, 176–7, 194, 199, 238, 239

cleaning routine 248–9

'as you go', cleaning 100–101

autumn simmer pot 265–6

baby oil 39–40, 50, 137, 148, 149, 151, 154

bad days 90–91

bags, wallets and purses 108–9

basic tasks, regular 17–18

bathroom 10–11, 13, 20, 24, 110, 123–44

bath 83, 129–30, 280, 282, 283, 285

bathmats 110, 139–40, 217

bath towels 138–9, 140, 283

bicarbonate of soda and 136, 138, 139

bins 135, 139

checklist 139–40, 142–3

chrome radiators 137, 140

cleaning kit and 32, 35, 43, 44, 48, 51, 52, 53, 54–5, 57, 59, 66

clutter hotspot 98

cupboards and surfaces 136–7

daily habits and 77, 79

extractor fan/vent 137–8

floors 137

four-week cleaning schedule and 83

light switch or cord 138

mirrors 135, 136

notes 141

bathroom – *cont.*
  plug holes 131
  quick cleaning tips 125
  quick five-minute cleans 135
  shower 127–31 *see also* shower
  sink and taps 126
  tile grouting 130
  toilet 131–6 *see also* toilet
  toothbrush 135, 136
  toothbrush holders 138
  walls 137
  weekly planner 144
beauty blenders 180, 181
bed bugs 44, 239–40
bedding 44, 84, 90, 116–17, 175,
    176–7, 180, 184, 185, 218, 239,
    281, 282, 283, 285, 286
  pet bedding 33–4, 241
bedroom 11, 18, 20, 45, 77, 79,
    173–90
  bedding and mattress *see*
    bedding
  beds 176
  brushes 180
  checklist 185 6, 188–9
  duvets and pillows 177–9
  four-week cleaning schedule
    and 83
  hairbrushes 183
  headboard 179–80
  how long to keep products 181–3
  kids' bedrooms 184–5
  make-up and beauty products
    180–83
  notes 187

quick cleaning tips 175
sponges or beauty blenders 181
weekly planner 190
wellbeing in 184
bicarbonate of soda 33–4, 39, 44,
    47, 50, 52, 130, 131, 136
  bathroom and 138, 139
  bedroom and 177, 183
  kitchen and 148, 149, 150, 151,
    154–61, 163–5
  laundry and ironing and 215
  living areas and 195, 199
  pests and 239, 241
  smelling fresh, keep your
    home 258, 262–4, 267
  stains and 244, 246–50
bins 17, 49, 83, 131, 135, 139, 153,
    155, 168, 235, 238, 268, 270,
    280, 281, 282, 284
blender or food processor 156, 168
blinds 56, 73, 83, 84, 85, 179, 185,
    186, 198, 201, 205, 281, 283,
    285, 288
blood stains 243
brooms 53
brushes 53, 180
  dish 55
  drain-cleaning 57
  hairbrush 163, 183, 186, 282
  make-up brushes 83, 137, 179,
    180, 186, 196, 202, 281, 283,
    285
  toilet 56–7, 83, 130, 132–4, 139,
    280
  toothbrush *see* toothbrush

caddy 58, 62, 285
candle wax 242, 245
chopping board 47, 84, 153, 155–6, 168, 283
Christmas simmer pot 265
chrome radiators 137, 140
citric acid 40
clove oil 44, 239
clutter *see* decluttering
cocktail sticks 58, 62, 151, 154, 195, 226, 263
coffee bean candle 258
coffee machine 47, 84, 153, 157, 168, 283
cooker hood 147, 164, 168, 284, 288
cooking utensils and appliances 109
cupboards 21, 31, 32, 53, 59, 66, 83, 84, 89, 234, 238, 269, 281, 283, 286
    bathroom 131, 136–7, 139
    decluttering and 97–100, 103, 104, 106–7, 108, 109
    kitchen 151–2, 153, 168
    living areas 203–4
    storage 106–7
curtains 56, 73, 83, 84, 179, 184, 186, 198, 200–201, 205, 220, 225, 239, 249, 258, 267, 281, 283, 285, 288
    net 217, 218
    shower 33, 44, 83, 129, 131, 140, 217, 280
cutlery 91, 107, 118, 159, 160, 161, 168

daily clean 57, 133, 163, 289
daily habits 2, 3, 11, 71–94, 125, 278
    ADHD, autism or neurodivergent conditions 91
    bad days 90–91
    bit by bit 76–7
    evening 77
    five habits 74
    four-week cleaning schedule 83–5
    general cleaning tips, three 85–6
    house rules 81–3
    lunchtime (if home) 77
    make it easy 75–6
    morning 77
    out all day 86–7
    parents and carers 88
    reduced mobility 89–90
    resetting 77–80
    tailor your habits 86
    take stock 75
    wind down 80–81
    working from home 87–8
declutter 3, 12, 67, 91, 95–122
    accessories 113
    as you go 100–101
    bags, wallets and purses 108–9
    bathroom 110, 136, 140
    bedding 116–17
    bedroom 116–17, 180, 182, 185, 186
    cleaning kit 108

declutter – *cont.*
  clutter hotspots 104–18
  cooking utensils and
    appliances 109–10
  declutter your life 118
  entrance way 115–16
  festive clean routine and 269
  food and 109
  four-week cleaning schedule
    and 84, 88
  four-week planner and 281–3
  fridge 110
  gift wrap supplies 117
  items to keep 105
  junk drawer 107
  kids' clothing 113–14
  kitchen 147, 152, 153, 154, 168
  living room 115
  one-in-one-out 99–100
  organisation tips for
    wardrobes 114
  paperwork 104–6
  shoes 113
  socks and underwear 113
  step back, take a 97–9
  storage cupboards 106–7
  thirty-day challenge 101–4,
    277, 286–8
  toys 110–11
  wardrobe 111–13
  work area 115
deep-cleaning 52, 55, 82, 83, 278,
  279
  bathroom 130, 132, 139
  bedroom 183

closets and drawers 236
  festive clean routine and 268,
    269, 270
  four-week planner 279–84
  kitchen 153, 156, 163, 168
  laundry and ironing 221, 223–4,
    226
  living areas 194, 195, 198–9, 205
  pushchair or highchair 247–8
  spring clean and clear
    challenge 287–8
delegating 66
denture tablets 47
descaling
  coffee machine 157
  kettle 15, 47, 84, 153, 158–9, 168,
    283, 287
  shower head 128, 140, 281
dish brush 55, 62
dish soap 32, 35, 37, 38, 46, 50, 52, 54
  bathroom 126, 127, 129, 130, 135,
    138
  bedroom 179
  kitchen 148, 149, 150, 151, 152,
    156, 158, 159, 166
  laundry and ironing and 213,
    215, 219
  living areas 194, 197, 199
  stains and 243–6
dishwasher 8, 10, 24, 47, 59, 77–9,
  87, 88, 89, 154, 155–6, 160–63,
  267, 278, 280, 282, 287
  loading 162
  surprising things you can put
    in to save time 162–3

disinfectant 17, 33, 45, 57, 83, 84, 85, 258, 264, 287, 288
  bathroom and 57, 83, 130, 131, 133–5, 138–40, 280, 281
  bedroom and 182–3, 185
  branded 41
  disinfecting and cleaning, difference between 41
  DIY disinfectant spray 24, 32–3, 35, 38, 39, 42, 50, 134, 202, 204, 238, 247, 248
  kitchen and 148, 150, 165
  living areas 84, 130, 198, 202, 203, 204, 205
  phone and electrical equipment 198, 202, 205, 284
  rubbing alcohol 34–8, 41–2, 50, 151, 154, 182, 185, 202, 203, 245–7
  sunlight 42
disposable wipes 58, 62
DIY sprays 130, 132, 137, 138, 148, 152, 156, 160, 184, 196, 225, 234, 240, 248–50, 258
  disinfectant spray 24, 32–3, 35, 38, 39, 42, 50, 134, 202, 204, 238, 247, 248
  dusting spray 36, 46, 50
  laminate floor cleaner 38, 50
drains 33, 46, 150, 168
  drain-cleaning brush 57, 62, 131
dryer balls 58, 62, 177, 222–3

dust 10, 11, 12, 17, 18, 23, 51, 52, 61, 65, 76, 81, 83, 84, 85, 89, 90, 109, 112, 238, 267, 269, 270
  allergies and 248–9
  bathroom 136–40
  bedroom 175, 176, 177, 179, 185–6
  defined 238
  DIY dusting spray 36, 46, 50
  dust mites 44, 60, 175, 176, 177, 237–8
  dusters 52–3, 62
  four-week planner 280–85
  kitchen 152–3, 163, 167
  living areas and 194–8, 200–201, 203, 204–5
  spring clean and clear challenge 287–8
duvets 116–17, 176, 177–80, 186, 217, 282, 288

electric or gas hob 163–4, 168
entrance way 10, 20, 115–16, 193, 198, 203–4, 269, 270, 281, 285, 286
essential oils 258, 259, 289
  bathroom and toilet and 131, 133, 135, 137
  bedroom and 176, 177
  cleaning kit and 33–8, 42, 43, 45, 46, 50
  guests and 267, 268
  keep your home smelling fresh tips and 264
  kitchen and 155

essential oils – *cont.*
   laundry and ironing and 223, 225
   living areas and 184, 195, 203
   pests and 235, 236, 237, 239–40
   scent bags and 262–3
   stains and 242, 250
eucalyptus 261–2
   oil 44
extractor fan/vent 125, 137–8, 140, 281, 287

fabric refresher 249–50, 258, 264
fabric softeners 33, 58, 139, 176, 212, 215, 216, 222–3
faeces 250
fake tan 247
festive clean routine 268–70
Five-Minute Clean Routine 7, 9–12, 17
   basic tasks 17–18
   bathroom and *see* bathroom
   bedroom and *see* bedroom
   benefits 16–17
   daily habits *see* daily habits
   decluttering and *see* decluttering
   early days of 17–18
   five-minute challenge 10–12
   flexibility of 15–16
   golden rule and 25
   kitchen and *see* kitchen
   laundry and ironing and *see* laundry and ironing
   living areas and *see* living areas

   momentum and 12–14
   pests and *see* pests
   pets and *see* pets
   questions to figure out what you want from your cleaning 18–25
   small wins 14–15
   special touches and *see* special touches
   stains and *see* stains
   toilet and *see* toilet
flexibility, Five-Minute Clean Routine and 15–16
floors
   allergies and 249
   bathroom and toilet 131, 134, 137, 140
   bedroom 179, 185, 186
   daily habits and 73, 77, 78, 83–4
   DIY laminate floor cleaner 38, 50
   festive clean routine and 269, 270
   five-minute challenge and 10, 11, 14, 17, 18, 20, 23
   four-week cleaning schedule 83, 84
   four-week planner 280–84
   guests and 267
   kitchen and 152, 153, 167, 168
   living areas and 194–6, 197, 198, 205
   pests and 234, 235
   products and 32, 33, 37, 48, 54, 55, 64, 67

food, decluttering and 109
four-week cleaning schedule 83–5
four-week planner 279–85
    Week 1 – Focus on bathroom
        280–81
    Week 2 – Focus on bedroom
        281–2
    Week 3 – Focus on kitchen
        282–4
    Week 4 – Focus on living areas
        284–5
fragrances 12, 34, 35, 37, 42, 195,
    203, 223, 257–60, 262, 263, 270
freezer 166
fridge 40, 47, 60, 151, 153, 154, 155,
    162, 168, 265, 269, 280, 282,
    283, 286, 287
    declutter 84, 110
    spray 37–8, 50

general cleaning tips, three 85–6
gift wrap supplies 106, 117
glass cleaner 34–6, 50, 137, 151–2,
    160
glass microfibre cloths 51–2, 126,
    127, 135, 148, 154
glasses 109, 160–61, 162, 268, 270,
    286
gloves, cleaning 57, 62, 249
golden rule 25
grapefruit oil 46
grass stain 243
grease and oil stains 244
guests 109, 110, 203, 233, 257,
    267–8

hairbrushes 163, 183–4, 186, 282
hard surfaces 83, 179, 185, 194, 196,
    204, 267, 270, 280, 281, 283
hard wood cleaner 38
headboard 56, 83, 179–80, 184,
    186, 239, 240, 268, 281
herbal simmer pot 266
hob 13, 52, 58, 59–60, 77, 79, 84,
    147, 150–51, 153, 159, 278, 282,
    284, 288
    electric or gas 163–4, 167, 168
    scraper 56, 62
House Rules 81–3
hydrogen peroxide (oxygen
    bleach) 40, 41, 50, 130, 143,
    243

ink stain 245
insects 24, 43, 44, 45, 75, 233, 234–
    5, 237, 239
ironing 80, 91, *214*, 224–6
items to keep 105

junk drawer 8, 107, 108, 286
junk mail 15, 74, 101, 105, 106, 286

kids
    bedrooms 11, 184–5
    clothing 113–14
kit, cleaning 31–2
    abrasive cleaning sponge 49
    all-purpose cleaner 35
    baby oil 39–40
    bicarbonate of soda 33–4
    brooms and brushes 53

kit, cleaning – *cont.*
  caddy 58
  checklist of tools 50–51
  citric acid 40
  cleaning gloves 57
  clove oil 44
  cocktail sticks 58
  denture tablets 47
  dish brush 55
  dish soap 32
  disinfectants, branded 41
  disinfectant spray 42
  disinfecting and cleaning,
    difference between 41
  disposable wipes 58
  DIY sprays 34–5
  drain-cleaning brush 57
  dryer balls 58
  dusters 52–3
  dusting spray 36
  essential oils 43–6
  eucalyptus oil 44
  flat-headed mop 54
  fridge spray 37
  glass and mirror cleaner 35–6
  glass microfibre cloths 52
  grapefruit oil 46
  hardwood cleaner 38
  hob scraper 56
  hydrogen peroxide (or oxygen
    bleach) 40–41
  laminate floor cleaner 38
  lavender oil 45
  lemon 46–7
  limescale removers 48

lint roller 56
microfibre cloths 51–2
mops 53–4
mould and mildew spray 36–7
moving, get 64–7
natural products 39
olive oil 46
orange and lemon oils 43–4
oxi powder 49
peppermint oil 45
power scrubber 59
power tools 58–9
pumice stone 56
rosemary oil 45
rubbing alcohol or surgical
  spirit 41
salt 46
safety 34, 39, 43
scourer 55
shaving foam 48
shop-bought products 48
soda crystals 39
sonic scrubber 59
speed up your cleaning, how to
  62–4
spin mop 54
spot carpet stain remover 49
spot cleaner 61
spray mop 54–5
squeegee 57
static dusters 53
steam cleaner 60
steam mop 55
stone surface cleaner 37
sunlight 42

tea tree oil 44
thyme oil 45
toilet brush 56–7
tools 51, 62
toothbrush 57–8
toothpaste 47
vacuum cleaner 61
white vinegar 33
window vacuum 59–60
kitchen 1, 10, 13, 18, 20, 23, 25, 32,
    35, 43, 54, 59–60, 63, 64, 75,
    78, 79, 145–72, 234, 238, 250,
    258, 264, 267
  air fryer 158
  bins 155
  blender or food processor 156
  checklist 167–8, 170–71
  chopping board 155–6
  coffee machine 157
  cooker hood 164
  cupboards 151–2
  cutlery 159
  decluttering and 286–7
  deep-cleaning jobs 163
  dishwasher 161–3
  drains 150
  electric or gas hob 163–4
  festive clean routine 269–70
  floors 152
  four-week cleaning schedule
    and 84
  four-week planner 279–84
  freezer 166
  fridge 154
  glasses 160

  hob 150–51
  kettle, descaling 158–9
  light fixtures 153
  microwave 158
  mugs 156–7
  notes 168–9
  order for washing up by hand
    161
  oven 164–5
  pots, pans and baking trays
    159–60
  quick cleaning tips 147
  quick five-minute cleans
    155–7
  sinks 149
  splashbacks 151
  spring clean and clear
    challenge 287–8
  taps 149
  toaster 156
  walls 152–3
  weekly planner 172
  windows 166–7
  worktops 148

laminate floor cleaner, DIY 38, 50
laundry 11, 13, 17–18, 32, 33, 45, 63,
    65, 76–7, 80, 82, 89, 91, 117,
    209–30, 243, 278
  checklist 226, 228–9
  deep-cleaning 223–4
  fabric softeners 222–3
  guide 214
  how often should you wash
    clothes? 216

laundry – *cont.*
how often should you wash
household items? 217
notes 227
pre-treating 213–16
speed up your washing routine
211–13
top tips 218
trainers 219
tumble dryer 222
washing machine 220–22
lavender oil 45
lemon 244, 259, 262–3, 264, 266
bathroom and toilet and 127, 131
cleaning tools and 35, 36, 37, 42,
43, 44, 46–7, 50
kitchen and 156, 158
laundry and 221–3
pests and 239, 242
light fixtures 153, 168, 186, 197,
205, 282, 284, 2287
limescale 33, 39, 40, 47, 56, 57,
125–8, 140, 149, 158, 222, 225
removers 48, 50, 128, 134
lint roller 56, 62, 179, 196, 198,
200, 212, 240
lipstick 181, 182, 242, 247
living areas 191–208
checklist 204–5, 207
curtains, blinds and shutters
200–201
declutter challenge and 286
entrance way and stairs 203–4
festive clean routine and 269,
270

floors 194–6
four-week cleaning schedule
and 84
four-week planner 279–85
hard surfaces 196
living room *see* living room
notes 206
quick cleaning tips 193
quick five-minute cleans 202
radiators 203
reset routine for 78–9
rubbing alcohol 203
sofa 198–200
walls 197–8
weekly planner 208
workspace 201–2
living room 10, 15, 18, 76–8, 88,
90, 101, 111, 115, 193, 194, 196,
200, 204, 269, 278

make-up and beauty products 83,
98, 110, 137, 175, 179, 180–83,
196, 202, 215, 242–3, 281, 283,
288
brushes 180
clean and disinfect 182–3
how long to keep products
181–2
sponges or beauty blenders 181
microfibre cloths 51–2, 54, 62,
80, 126, 127, 129, 133, 135–7,
148–51, 153, 154, 160, 164, 165,
196–202, 217
microwave 47, 81, 84, 153, 158, 162,
168, 283

mildew 33, 36–7, 44, 45, 50, 125, 128, 130–31, 137–8, 140, 177, 220, 264, 288

mirrors 10, 48, 52, 57, 59, 83, 131, 135, 136, 139, 186, 197, 267, 269, 270, 280, 282, 284

cleaner 35–6, 50

mobility, reduced 22, 24, 59, 89–90

momentum 12–14

mop 2, 3, 17, 18, 23, 25, 31, 37, 38, 53–5, 65–6, 83–4, 99, 125, 131, 134, 139, 140, 168, 179, 185, 186, 196, 198, 204, 205, 217, 220, 234, 235, 249, 270

Flash Speed Mop 53, 137, 153, 197

flat-headed mop 51, 54, 62, 106, 137, 152–3, 155, 166, 194, 197

four-week planner 280–84

spin mop 54, 127, 129, 136, 194

spray mop 54–5, 147, 152, 155

spring clean and clear challenge and 287, 288

steam mop 55, 195

moths 236–7

mould 33, 36–7, 44, 45, 48, 50, 110, 125, 127, 128–31, 137–8, 140, 177–8, 180–81, 220, 260, 264, 288

moving, get 64–7

mud stain 244

mugs 46, 47, 91, 109, 156–7, 161, 162, 168, 286

nail polish 245, 246, 247

natural products 39, 49, 241, 248, 262

olive oil 36, 46, 50, 148

one-in-one-out 99–101, 105

orange and lemon oils 43–4

out all day 86–7

oven 17, 33, 40, 52, 55, 57, 59, 75, 105, 162, 164–5, 168, 220, 284, 287

oxi powder 49, 51, 215

paperwork 87, 103, 104–6, 115

parents and carers 88

peppermint oil 45, 235, 237, 239, 241–2, 262, 263

pests 24, 45, 233–40

pets 21, 22, 24, 34, 43, 45, 56, 60, 177, 199, 233, 235, 236, 237, 240–42, 249, 259

pillows 49, 67, 81, 116–17, 176–9, 184, 186, 194, 197, 200, 217, 219, 282, 288

plants, flowers and herbs 260–66

plug holes 83, 84, 131, 140, 153, 281, 283

pomander balls 263

pots, pans and baking trays 159–60

power scrubber 59

power tools 25, 31, 58–9, 91

pre-treating 213–16

pumice stone 56, 62, 134
pushchairs and highchairs 247–8

quick cleaning tips 125, 147, 175,
    193, 257, 277
quick five-minute cleans 135,
    155–7, 202, 238–9

radiators 137, 140, 203, 205, 264,
    281, 285, 288
red wine 48, 242, 245
reduced mobility 22, 24, 59,
    89–90
reed diffuser 259, 267
resetting 11, 15, 77–80, 147, 193,
    194, 278, 279
rewards, cleaning and 2, 7, 9,
    14–15, 16, 66–7, 86, 257
rodents 233, 237
rosemary oil 45
rubbing alcohol 34, 35, 36, 37, 38,
    41–2, 50, 151, 154, 182, 185,
    202, 203, 245, 246, 247

salt 46, 50
safety 34, 39, 43, 61, 66, 221,
    223
scent bags 12, 49, 236, 261,
    262–3, 268
scourer 46, 55, 62, 129, 148, 160,
    164, 165
shame 14, 104, 164
shaving foam 48
shoes 80, 82, 113, 114, 115, 204, 238,
    269

shop-bought products 48
shower 17, 44, 46, 54, 55, 99, 125,
    127–9, 249, 260, 261, 270,
    280, 282, 283
    curtain 44, 63, 129, 131, 140,
        217, 280
    head 33, 59, 128, 140, 262,
        281
    hose 128–9
    limescale 127, 128
    mould and mildew 128, 130–31
    screen 10, 11, 52, 57, 59, 127, 130,
        135, 139, 140, 285
simmer pots 12, 91, 265, 266, 270
sink and taps 24
    bathroom 125, 126–7, 128, 129,
        131, 135, 139
    cleaning habits and 76, 77, 78,
        79, 83, 84
    cleaning kit and 39–40, 47, 48,
        55, 57, 59, 63
    festive clean routine 273
    five-minute challenge and
        10–11
    four-week planner 280–82,
        284
    kitchen 147, 149, 153, 156, 165,
        167, 281, 284
small wins 2, 9, 14–15, 67, 289
smelling fresh, tips for ways to
    keep your home 264
socks and underwear 113, 213, 216,
    287
soda crystals 39, 50, 132, 150,
    215–16, 221

sofa 11, 18, 61, 76, 79, 82, 84, 193, 194, 198–200, 204, 205, 267, 268, 269, 282, 283, 284, 285
sonic scrubber 59
special touches 257–74
  air freshener 258
  checklist 272–3
  coffee bean candle 258
  eucalyptus 261–2
  fabric refresher 258
  festive clean routine 268–70
  fragrances 257–8
  guests 267–8
  notes 271
  plants, flowers and herbs 260–61
  pomander balls 263
  quick cleaning tips 257
  quick five-minute wins 260
  reed diffuser 259
  scent bags 262–3
  simmer pots 265–6
  smelling fresh, tips for ways to keep your home 264
  wax melt 259
  weekly planner 274
speed up your cleaning 62–4
speed up your washing routine 211–13
spiders 44, 45, 235–6
spin mop 54, 127, 129, 136, 194
splashbacks 84, 151, 153, 168, 269, 280, 283, 284, 287

sponges 51, 55, 108, 149, 151, 157, 159, 163–4, 181, 186, 212, 242, 283, 285
spot carpet stain remover 49, 50
spot cleaner 61
spray mop 54–5
spring and summer simmer pot 266
spring clean and clear challenge 287–8
squeegee 57, 62, 99, 125, 127, 139, 163, 166, 167
stains 12, 109, 110, 113, 177, 242–8, 270, 285
  bathroom and toilet 127, 132, 133, 134
  blood 243
  candle wax 245
  daily habits and 84, 85, 91
  fake tan 247
  grass 243
  grease and oil 244
  ink 245
  kitchen 148, 149, 151, 154, 156, 159, 160, 163, 164, 165, 168
  laundry and 213–15, 219, 225
  lipstick 247
  living areas 195, 198, 199, 200
  mud 244
  nail polish 245
  products and 32, 33, 39, 40, 41, 42, 46, 47, 48, 49, 50, 55, 56, 59, 61
  pushchairs and highchairs 247–8

stains – *cont.*
  red wine 245
  stickers 246
  suncream 244
  tomato or ketchup 244–5
  Tupperware 46
  urine 250
  wall marks 246
  water rings 246
static dusters 53
steam cleaning/steam cleaner 51,
    60, 62
  bathroom and toilet and
    133
  four-week planner 285
  kitchen and 148, 151, 154
  living areas and 195, 196,
    199, 200, 201, 203,
    205
  moths and 236
  spring clean and clear
    challenge 288
  stains 245, 248, 249
steam mop 55, 195
step back, take a 97–9
stickers 246
stone surface cleaner 37, 50
storage 21, 88, 99, 106–7, 114, 115,
    116, 175, 185, 193, 201, 203–4,
    262, 286
stress 14, 15, 20, 65, 76, 80, 118,
    212, 222
suncream 42, 136, 244
sunlight 42

taps 9, 12, 15, 33, 40, 47, 48,
    57, 83, 84, 126, 129, 131,
    139, 149, 153, 167, 280, 281,
    282, 284
tea tree oil 36, 44, 129, 130
thirty-day challenge 101–4
thyme oil 45
'tidy up' tune 66
tile grouting 33, 40, 44, 57, 59, 130,
    140, 281
toaster 10, 84, 153, 156, 168, 269,
    283, 288
toilet 10, 17, 24, 123–44, 257–8,
    260, 270, 278, 288
  brush 56–7, 62, 83, 130, 132–3,
    134, 139, 280
  cleaning kit 39, 40, 47, 48, 49,
    56–7, 59, 60, 62
  daily clean 133
  daily habits 77, 79
  deep-clean 132–3, 270, 280, 281,
    283, 284
  flushing 136
  four-week cleaning schedule
    83
  four-week planner and 280
  steam clean 133
  top tips 134
tomato or ketchup stains
    244–5
tools
  checklist 62
  cleaning 51
  power 58–9

toothbrush 44, 47, 57–8, 59, 62,
    83, 126, 128, 129, 130, 131, 132,
    136, 139, 149, 164, 167, 183,
    220, 221, 226, 244, 245, 246,
    247, 250
    disinfecting 83, 131, 135, 140, 281
    holders 138, 163, 239
toothpaste 24, 47, 50, 126, 150,
    165, 220, 221, 222, 226, 246
toys 56, 88, 102, 110–11, 162, 184–5,
    186, 194, 204, 220, 241, 286
trainers 47, 49, 97, 219–20,
    264
tumble dryer 42, 49, 52, 58, 177,
    222, 223, 225, 226, 239, 285
Tupperware 80, 97, 109, 246, 286

urine 49, 134, 248, 250

vacuum cleaner 17, 18, 23, 34, 37,
    61, 64–5, 67, 77, 88, 89, 90,
    112, 233, 234, 237, 238, 239,
    240, 247, 248–50, 264, 267
    bathroom and toilet 137, 138,
    139, 140
    bedroom 176–7, 178–80, 185,
    186
    festive clean routine 269, 270,
    278
    five-minute challenge and
    10–11
    four-week cleaning schedule
    84
    four-week planner 280–85

kitchen 147, 148, 151, 152, 166, 167
laundry 222, 223, 224
living areas 193, 194–6, 198,
    199, 200, 201, 203, 204–5
window vacuum 23, 57,
    59–60, 62, 127, 139, 147, 148,
    151, 166
vomit 249–50

walls
    bathroom 131, 137, 139
    bedroom 186
    cleaning kit and 47, 49, 53, 54
    daily habits and 83, 84
    kitchen 152–3, 168
    living areas 194, 197–8, 204, 205
    marks on 246
    mopping 131, 280, 282, 284, 287
wardrobes 99, 100, 111–14, 116,
    211–12, 232, 261, 268, 287
    organisation tips 114
washing machine 108, 129, 200,
    241, 247, 281, 288
    bedroom and 178, 182, 185
    laundry and 211, 212, 215, 216,
    218–22, 226
    products 39, 44–5, 47, 54
water rings 46, 246
wax 242, 245, 259
wellbeing, bedroom and 184
white vinegar 234
    bathroom and 126–31, 134, 135,
    137, 138, 139
    bedroom 176

white vinegar – *cont.*
  cleaning kit and 33, 35, 36, 37,
    38, 41, 46, 50
  kitchen 149, 150, 152, 156–7,
    159, 160, 161, 164, 166
  laundry and 212, 213, 215, 216,
    218, 221, 225
  stains and 243, 244, 245, 247,
    250, 258, 264
wind down 80–81, 175, 194
windows 18, 20, 23, 33, 62, 64–6
  bathroom 127, 139
  bedroom 180
  cleaning kit and 41, 45, 52, 54,
    56, 57, 59–60, 166–7
  daily habits and 76, 82, 84,
    86, 90
  festive clean routine and
    268–70
  four-week planner and 281–4
  guests and 267

insects and 234, 235, 238
  kitchen 147, 148, 151, 166–7, 168
  living areas 198, 200, 205
  spring clean and clear
    challenge 288
  window vacuum 23, 57,
    59–60, 62
wins
  quick five-minute 260
  small 2, 9, 14–15, 67, 289
work area/workspace 115,
    201–2, 281–2
working from home 2, 16, 64,
    87–8, 115
worktops 8, 10, 17, 238, 267, 269,
    278, 287
  cleaning kit and 32, 33, 37, 40,
    51, 59–60
  daily habits and 75, 77, 78, 79,
    87, 88
  kitchen 147, 148, 149, 151, 167